101 Life Skills Games
for Children

Other Smart Fun Books

101 Music Games for Children by Jerry Storms
101 More Music Games for Children by Jerry Storms
101 Dance Games for Children by Paul Rooyackers
101 More Dance Games for Children by Paul Rooyackers
101 Drama Games for Children by Paul Rooyackers
101 More Drama Games for Children by Paul Rooyackers
101 Movement Games for Children by Huberta Wiertsema
101 Language Games for Children by Paul Rooyackers
101 Improv Games for Children by Bob Bedore
101 Life Skills Games for Children by Bernie Badegruber
101 More Life Skills Games for Children by Bernie Badegruber
101 Cool Pool Games for Children by Kim Rodomista
101 Family Vacation Games by Shando Varda
101 Relaxation Games for Children by Allison Bartl
101 Quick-Thinking Games + Riddles for Children by Allison Bartl
101 Pep-Up Games for Children by Allison Bartl
404 Deskside Activities for Energetic Kids by Barbara Davis, MA, MFA
Yoga Games for Children by Danielle Bersma and Marjoke Visscher
The Yoga Adventure for Children by Helen Purperhart
The Yoga Zoo Adventure by Helen Purperhart
Yoga Exercises for Teens by Helen Purperhart

Ordering

Trade bookstores in the U.S. and Canada, please contact:

Publishers Group West
1700 Fourth Street, Berkeley CA 94710
Phone: (800) 788-3123   Fax: (800) 351-5073

Hunter House books are available at bulk discounts for course adoptions; to qualifying community, health-care, and government organizations; and for special promotions and fund-raising. For details please contact:

Special Sales Department
Hunter House Inc., PO Box 2914, Alameda CA 94501-0914
Phone: (510) 865-5282   Fax: (510) 865-4295
E-mail: ordering@hunterhouse.com

Individuals can order our books from most bookstores, by calling toll-free **(800) 266-5592**, or from our website at **www.hunterhouse.com**

101
Life Skills Games
Children

Learning, Growing, Getting Along
(Ages 6 to 12)

Bernie Badegruber

A Hunter House SmartFun book

Hunter House Inc., Publishers
PO Box 2914
Alameda CA 94501-0914

Library of Congress Cataloging-in-Publication Data

Badegruber, Bernd.
   [Spiele zum Problemlösen. Band 1. English]
   101 life skills games for children : learning, growing, getting along (ages 6 to 12) / Bernie Badegruber.-- 1st ed.
      p. cm.
   Includes index.
   Summary: "Collection of games aimed at enhancing children's self-awareness and social and emotional skills, helping them understand and deal with problems in daily interactions with other children and adults"--Provided by publisher.
   ISBN-13: 978-0-89793-441-1 (pbk.)
   ISBN-10: 0-89793-441-5 (pbk.)
   ISBN-13: 978-0-89793-442-8 (spiral bound)
   ISBN-10: 0-89793-442-3 (spiral bound)
   1. Social skills--Study and teaching--Activity programs. 2. Life skills--Study and teaching--Activity programs. 3. Educational games. I: Title: One hundred one life skills games for children. II. Title: One hundred and one life skills games for children. III. Title.
   LB1139.S6B321913 2005   2003012860

Project Credits

Cover Design: Jil Weil & Stefanie Gold
Illustration: Alois Jesner — Graphikdesign
Book Production: Rachel Reiss & Hunter
   House
Translator: Elisabeth Wohofsky
Developmental Editors: Alexandra Palmer
   and Peter Schneider
Copy Editor: Peter Schneider
Acquisitions Editor: Jeanne Brondino
Editor: Alexandra Mummery

Publishing Assistants: Antonia T. Lee,
   Herman Leung
Publicist: Jillian Steinberger
Publishing Intern: Shelley McGuire
Customer Service Manager: Christina
   Sverdrup
Order Fulfillment: Washul Lakdhon,
   Joe Winebarger
Administrator: Theresa Nelson
Computer Support: Peter Eichelberger
Publisher: Kiran S. Rana

Printed and bound by Bang Printing, Brainerd, Minnesota
Manufactured in the United States of America

11 10 9 8 7 6   First Edition   12 13 14 15 16

Contents

Preface   xi

Introduction

Thoughts on Playing with Children   1

Play Therapy and Game Pedagogy   3

How to Use This Book   4

A Brief Word on Brevity   5

Key to the Icons Used in the Games   5

I Games

What I Like   10

What I Can Do   18

What I Observe   21

You Games

Getting to Know You   40

Understanding You   49

Working with You   55

We Games

Warming-up Games for the Group   66

Cooperation Games.   72

Integrating New Classmates   83

Helping Games   93

Aggression Games   120

Adding More Imagination

Statue and Sculpting Games. 146

Fairytale Games 159

Pantomime Play 167

Keyword Index 173

A detailed list of the games indicating
appropriate group sizes begins on the next page.

Index of Games

Page	Game	pairs	groups of 3	groups of 4	any size

I Games

What I Like

Page	Game	pairs	groups of 3	groups of 4	any size
10	I Like This Picture				•
12	The Run-to Game				•
14	Wishing Cards				•
16	Evil Fairy's Hat				•
17	Good Fairy				•

What I Can Do

Page	Game	pairs	groups of 3	groups of 4	any size
18	I Can, I Can't				•
19	Guess What I Can Do				•

What I Observe

Page	Game	pairs	groups of 3	groups of 4	any size
21	Observing the Room				•
23	The Room's ABCs				•
25	Changing the Room				•
26	What's Made of This?				•
28	The Traveling Mystery				•
30	A Piece at a Time				•
31	Seeing with Your Ears				•
32	Telling Noises Apart				•
34	Stand Up for Your Instrument				•
35	Telling Sounds Apart				•
36	Collecting Sound Qualities				•
38	Song Memory				•

You Games

Getting to Know You

Page	Game	pairs	groups of 3	groups of 4	any size
40	Traveling Names				•
42	Crossword Puzzle Names				•

	pairs	groups of 3	groups of 4	any size

Page Game

		pairs	groups of 3	groups of 4	any size
43	Gathering Names				•
44	Autograph Book				•
45	Building Names				•
46	Mirror Names				•
47	The Seat on My Right Is Empty (with a Twist)				•

Understanding You

		pairs	groups of 3	groups of 4	any size
49	I Met My Match				•
50	You Sculpt Me	•			
51	You Reflect Me	•			
52	You Draw Me	•			
53	You Move Me	•			
54	When It Rains, It Pours	•			

Working with You

		pairs	groups of 3	groups of 4	any size
55	Holding Me with Your Eyes	•			
56	Helping Hands	•			
57	Picking Up Sticks Together	•			
58	New World Record	•			
59	Dance Partners	•			
60	Patty-Cake	•			
61	Twins				•
63	Fair Ball		•		

We Games

Warming-up Games for the Group

		pairs	groups of 3	groups of 4	any size
66	Balloon Dance				•
67	That Seat's Taken				•
69	Greeting Game				•
70	Good Morning!				•

Cooperation Games

		pairs	groups of 3	groups of 4	any size
72	Together on One Chair				•
74	Take a Bow				•
76	Boom Box				•

Page	Game	pairs	groups of 3	groups of 4	any size
78	Beat the Clock				•
79	Building Skyscrapers				•
80	Tug of War				•
81	Paper Streamer				•

Integrating New Classmates

Page	Game	pairs	groups of 3	groups of 4	any size
83	Wake Up!				•
85	The Grouping Game				•
87	Hot Seat				•
89	I'm Here!				•
91	Information Please				•

Helping Games

Page	Game	pairs	groups of 3	groups of 4	any size
93	Solution Memory				•
96	The Comforter Game				•
98	The Helper Game				•
100	Friendly Exam				•
102	Cry for Help				•
104	Emergency Kit				•
105	I Fell in the Well				•
107	Bodyguards				•
109	Brother, Help! Sister, Help!				•
111	Freeze Tag				•
112	Crocodile Tears				•
114	Moving Help				•
116	Carrying Contest	•			
118	First Day of School				•

Aggression Games

Page	Game	pairs	groups of 3	groups of 4	any size
120	Animals in the Jungle				•
122	Tug of War II				•
123	I-You-We Dice				•
126	Slo-Mo Tennis				•
128	Polite Wild Animals				•
130	Detective				•
132	Frontline	•			
134	Peace Language			•	

Page	Game	pairs	groups of 3	gourps of 4	any size
136	Rumors				•
138	Praise				•
139	Ghosts and Travelers				•
141	Vampire				•
143	Wolf in Sheep's Clothing				•

Adding More Imagination

Statue and Sculpting Games

Page	Game	pairs	groups of 3	gourps of 4	any size
146	Frozen Elves				•
147	Spin and Freeze				•
148	Frozen Music				•
149	Statue Pairs	•			
151	Mannequins				•
153	Wax Museum				•
154	Class Picture				•
156	Acting Out Pictures				•
157	Human Slide Show				•

Fairytale Games

Page	Game	pairs	groups of 3	gourps of 4	any size
159	Bad News and Good News Pairs	•			
161	Fairytale Personalities	•			
163	Fairytale Surprises				•
165	Living in a Fairytale				•

Pantomime Play

Page	Game	pairs	groups of 3	gourps of 4	any size
167	Getting Stronger				•
168	Unpacking a Gift				•
169	Waiter				•
170	Flying Masks				•
171	Mime Chain				•

Preface

What are life skills? Aside from the practical skills required for getting on in life, children need to develop social and emotional skills in order to become well-adjusted adults. These skills are the focus of this book.

In particular, the games in this book and in *101 More Life Skills Games for Children* (for children and teens aged 9–15) are designed to foster competence and awareness in the following areas: self-awareness, self-regulation of emotions, active listening, verbal and nonverbal communication, collaboration with others in pairs and larger groups, and observing and understanding other people's feelings. These are essential skills, the building blocks of a successful life. Participating in the games in this book in class or at a camp will help a child to develop in a safe and supportive environment.

We considered calling these areas of social and emotional development *life values* rather than life skills but didn't want to mislead readers into assuming that we are recommending moral principles or prescribing what is right and wrong. Rather, the focus is on developing the foundation skills of self-awareness and getting along with others. Once these foundations are in place, children are equipped to learn the skills required to become independent. These are addressed in other books and are likely to be of more value when your children are a little older.

School counselors and teachers have noted an increase in the number of children who have difficulties assimilating into the classroom environment. To help these children, counselors have to rely on strong participation from parents, teachers, educators, and other adults. This book has been created to help them.

Children who have problems in the classroom have a tendency to cause problems for others, too. These children need models for developing social and problem-solving skills. In a structured group they can experience and try out social behavior. They can learn through daily practice and contact with other children. Make-believe situations can help—in make-believe children can find security. With the games in this book, while having fun, children can deal with a current conflict in the classroom or with a make-believe problem that will help prepare them for real-life situations in the future.

Life skills games can also work at the group level, so that group members can face future problems with confidence and develop problem-solving competence as a group. A child who feels safe in a strong group will also be better at facing problems outside the group.

The games in this book are arranged in four sections, according to the ways in which they achieve their goals.

In *I Games,* the communication is mostly one-way. The main skill targeted here is for children to explore themselves and express what they observe. Of course, the children listen to what others have to say, but there is no group reflection about what has been said: no questions asked, no comments made.

You Games focus on how children perceive a partner. They try to learn more about the partner through observation, questioning, responding, commenting, and mirroring. Doing this, they learn a bit more about themselves but also get closer to another person, and then to more and more members of the group.

We Games emphasize the goals of learning to orient oneself in a group, knowing one's position within the group, and recognizing and using the strengths and weaknesses of group members and of the group itself. Children might also learn that a group changes, i.e., that the characteristics of a group fluctuate. Positions, relationships, moods, and potential in a group are partially stable, partially dependent on the situation.

In *We Games,* members of a group learn to recognize differences between their own and other groups, and how to assess and accept other groups.

As the children get better at the earlier games in the book, the group leader can introduce them to the games in the fourth section, *Adding More Imagination*. These games have fewer rules and allow for more creativity.

In each of the four sections, many of the games have "Reflections" and "Role Play" suggestions. The Reflections are examples of questions the leader can ask the children in order to maximize the possibilities for learning and discussion opened up by the games. The Role Play suggestions add another dimension to the games by enabling the players to encounter each other "in character."

We have alternated the use of male and female pronouns throughout the book. Of course, every "he" could be a "she," and every "her" could just as easily be "his."

Introduction

Thoughts on Playing with Children

What Makes an Activity "Play"?

An activity that is engaged in for its own sake—or just because it's fun—is considered play. Play is about the joy of doing something. In play, earning a living and struggling for survival take a back seat—in fact, results of any kind are of only minor importance. Another characteristic of play is that a game may have an almost infinite number of variations; no one minds if the rules of a game are changed—as long as everyone agrees to it! Variations offer children ways to experiment, to try new experiences and to learn to cope with their environment. Of course, there always needs to be a balance between experimenting and following the rules. This book tries to maintain that balance.

From these thoughts about play, I have derived the following five characteristics that a game should have in order to qualify as play.

The Five Characteristics of Play

1. It doesn't have a clear purpose that children are aware of
If a child doesn't realize that he is supposed to learn something from an activity, the activity is play. Concepts like "learning games" and "playful work" exist only in the adult mind. By controlling the goal, an adult can turn a child's game into "work" without the child realizing it. That is, the adult knows that the child learns from playing (that the play has a purpose), but the child doesn't have to worry about it.

2. It must be voluntary
Play is voluntary. You can stop whenever you want. Nobody can be forced to play a game. The other players may look down on somebody who doesn't want to participate or who quits, but that's all. A teacher or group leader should never force anyone to play a game!

3. The rules are flexible
In an individual or group game, the rules can be changed any time as long

as the new rules are understood by all. Changing, adapting, or even inventing new rules fosters intelligence and creativity.

4. It evokes emotional responses that are short-lived

By emotional responses, I mean intense feelings of joy, expectation, hope, anger, fear, relief, uncertainty, happiness, a sense of belonging, aggression, and so on. On the one hand, these feelings can be intense; on the other hand, they can be defused by the thought that "It's just a game." This is a way of learning to deal with tensions constructively. Indeed, if an activity has no tension built into it, a child might not even consider it to be a game—it might feel more like an exercise or merely an activity.

Some of the games in this book can be used as life skills exercises rather than life skills games. This form of social learning is also meaningful, but it's not play, and the leader must be aware of the difference.

5. It benefits from experimentation

A game is perhaps more of a game when there are several ways to play it. There can be different play tactics, goals, and rule interpretations. Experimenting is an opportunity to learn something new. Games that contain multiple possibilities for experimenting, inventing, and creativity are "learning games" in the best possible sense.

Goals of Games

For more information on any of the psychological theories behind how certain goals are achieved in these games, consult the psychologists listed in parentheses below:

Experimenting and experiencing of functions (Jean Piaget)

Practicing and automating (Jean Piaget, G. Stanley Hall, Karl Groos)

Learning and practicing rules (Jean Piaget)

Dealing with drives (G. Stanley Hall)

Experiencing and exerting power (Alfred Adler)

Catharsis (purification) (Sigmund Freud)

Cognitive learning (Jean Piaget)

Activation (Heinz Heckhausen)

Conserving excess energy (Herbert Spencer)

Play Therapy and Game Pedagogy

The purpose of this book is to offer educators a group of games that help them in their work with children. For the children, the games are a way to have fun. For the group leader, they are something more: a way to help children to understand and learn to cope in a game setting with conflicts and problems that might become all too real in the future. It is *not* the job of the game leader to deal with problems and conflicts from a child's past—that task should be left to a therapist. However, the fact that this book doesn't have a primarily therapeutic purpose doesn't mean that it can't be used by therapists in their work.

The following quote paraphrases the Swiss psychologist Hans Zullinger (H. Glotze and W. Jaede. *Die nicht-direktive Spieltherapie* [Non-Directive Game Therapy]), whose definition of a game is closest to my own:

> For Zullinger, the child is healed through the game itself; the therapist intervenes whenever there is a possibility of actively pushing ahead and developing the game further. The therapist can add his or her own impetus (in Zullinger's sense), produce material and arrange and structure a situation in a way he or she considers right. Thus the child is offered opportunities to use games to reduce emotional tensions and solve social conflicts. With the help of the therapist as game partner and through independent activities, these activities become increasingly constructive. In other words, Zullinger preferred pure game therapy—don't interpret for the child, but offer a great deal of variety of games and game practices.

The Role of the Group Leader

In the following quote, Jürgen Fritz (J. Fritz, *Methoden des sozialen Lernens* [Methods of Social Learning]) quotes Benita Daublensky's tips (B. Daublensky, *Spielen in der Schule* [Playing in School]) on the best ways for a group leader to achieve optimal results in games:

- Realize that you are not doing the children a favor.
- Help individuals without making them dependent on you.
- Protect children from difficulty without being overprotective. Let them create their own experiences as much as possible.
- Allow children to arrange themselves in pairs or groups as they wish, but help those who don't get chosen.

- Keep competition between children to a minimum.
- Create an open atmosphere and demonstrate to the children how they can help each other.

How to Use This Book

First Way: Going Step-By-Step

The games start with *I Games*. You can play some or all of the *I Games*, followed by *You Games*, and then *We Games*. Warm-up games for the group (listed in the index under "warming-up") can always be played at the beginning or in between the games. As children get better at the games in the first three sections, they can be introduced to the games in the last section, *Adding More Imagination*.

Second Way: Focusing on a Specific Problem

After a few warm-up games, start with any section that speaks to your concerns at the moment.

Example: You begin with the "Aggression Games" as a way to approach the subject of aggression. Afterward, you look at it from a preventive perspective by playing "Helping Games," "Cooperation Games," or games for "Integrating New Classmates."

Third Way: Using the Follow-up Games

At the end of each game you will find suggestions for follow-up games. They either lead you to the games on the neighboring pages of the book or to games that have similar goals, playing methods, or player configurations.

Examples: You go from a partner game to another partner game. You go from setting a world record with a partner in New World Record (Game #36) to imitating a partner's dance movements in Dance Partners (Game #37). After a conversation game, you compare that game to a pantomime game. After a partner observation game, you play other perception games.

You can play the follow-up games in the given order. Alternatively, you can stick with any follow-up game you like and pursue the follow-up suggestions given there, going further off from the starting point while your game program gains variety.

A Brief Word on Brevity

If you're used to reading game instructions, you may be surprised that the ones in this book are so short. There is a reason for it.

When a group leader sticks too closely to a game's rules, following detailed playing instructions, his dependence on the rules can communicate itself to the group—to the detriment of all. In this book, I try to suggest games instead of prescribing them. Be too specific tends to limit the players and does not stimulate their creativity.

What if you, the game leader, don't completely understand the variations of a game? In that case, you will probably create your own variations—and that is as it should be. In my teacher-training seminars, I often give instructions that are intentionally brief. Inexperienced game players are often temporarily at a loss, but, necessity being the mother of invention, they soon begin to try out their own interpretations. When they ask "Now do we have to...?" or "Can we...?" I simply shrug—and watch their questions disappear as new games get created.

Not all eventualities and possibilities can be covered in a book such as this. Different groups will reach different ideas in different ways, all of them unpredictable. In my seminars, I usually play the basic version before I encourage students to invent alternate ones.

The approach and games in *101 Life Skills Games for Children* can be combined well with the principles of "open learning," about which much has been written elsewhere.

Key to the Icons Used in the Games

To help you find games suitable for a particular situation, the games are coded with symbols or icons. These icons tell you, at a glance, the following things about the game:

- the size of the group needed
- the level of difficulty
- if a large space is needed
- if music is required
- if props are required
- if physical contact is or might be involved

These icons are explained in more detail below. Two icons included in other SmartFun books (age level and time) have been omitted here because the age group in this book is already clearly defined as children ages 6–12 (exercises for children ages 9–15 can be found in *101 More Life Skills Games for Children*) and because the duration of each game will vary depending on a number of factors including the size of the group and whether or not the particular game appeals to the players.

The size of the group needed. Most of the games are best played by a large group of players. If a game requires an even number of players, groups of 4, and so on, the game will be marked with the appropriate icon:

 = Even number

 = Groups of 3

 = Groups of 4

 = Game is suitable for a group of any size

The level of difficulty. The more complex games in this book that might be suited to older players are marked with the following icon:

 = For advanced players

If a large space is needed. Almost every game in this book can be played in a classroom. The few games that require a larger space, such as a gym, are marked with the following icon:

 = Large space needed

If music is required. Only a few games in this book require recorded music. If the music is optional, it is noted as such; if it is required, the icon below is used:

 = Music required

If props are required. Many of the games require no special props. In some cases, though, items such as chairs, instruments, paper and pens, or other materials are integral to running and playing a game. Games requiring props are flagged with the icon below, and the necessary materials are listed under the Props heading. Note that optional props will also be flagged (except when optional background music is the only item listed).

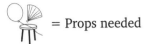 = Props needed

If physical contact is or might be involved. Although a certain amount of body contact might be acceptable in certain environments, the following icon has been inserted at the top of any exercises that might involve anywhere from a small amount of contact to minor collisions. You can figure out in advance if the game is suitable for your participants and/or environment.

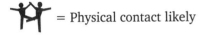 = Physical contact likely

I Games

What I Like
Games 1–5

What I Can Do
Games 6–7

What I Observe
Games 8–19

I Like This Picture

Props: Assorted pictures from magazines (enough for all players); a small table; chairs for all players (optional); soft background music (optional)

Goals
Developing a self-image
Improving the ability to introduce oneself

How to Play: Chairs are arranged in a circle, with a small table in the center. On the table are many postcard-sized pictures of things like houses, a butterfly, a princess, a table with place settings, the sun, and so forth. Everyone takes a turn choosing a picture and, after introducing herself, explains why she likes it. A player may choose a picture that has already been chosen by another player.

Examples
- "My name is Lisa. I chose the picture of the sun because I like to lie in the sun."
- "My name is Thomas, and I also chose the picture of the sun because it reminds me of our vacation in Italy."

Variation: At the beginning, everybody walks around the pictures, which have been scattered on the floor, while soft music is playing in the background.

Note: It is not very difficult or embarrassing for children to say what they like when they're simply describing a picture—it's much easier than talking about oneself. With groups in which children know each other's names, the name introduction can be omitted. If there is a new child in the group, however, this game can be played as an introduction game.

Reflections

- Does anyone in the group like similar things?
- Was it difficult for anyone to choose a picture?

Follow-up Games

1–19: I Games ◆ 20–26: Getting to Know You ◆ 41–44: Warming-up Games for the Group ◆ 52–56: Integrating New Classmates

The Run-to Game

Goals

- Remembering names
- Making contacts
- Warming up to a group

How to Play: After the players take turns introducing themselves, the leader asks one player to make a statement that describes another person

(the statement should be neutral or positive, not hurtful). The others try to guess who the statement is about, and when they think they've figured it out they run to that person as fast as they can and shake her hand. The first person to get there is the winner and gets to make the next statement.

Examples
- "His name is Martin."
- "Her hair is long and blond."

Variation: After introducing themselves to each other, everybody walks around. The statement is presented while people walk around.

Note: The children should be careful not to bump into each other when they start running. To encourage calm behavior, make a rule that if players bump into each other, they have to sit down until the next statement is announced.

Follow-up Games
4: Evil Fairy's Hat ◆ 7: Guess What I Can Do

3

What I Like

Wishing Cards

Props: Assorted pictures from magazines (enough for all players)

Goals

- Expressing wishes
- Fulfilling wishes
- Being generous
- Learning to do without
- Learning that wishes can be deferred

How to Play: After playing I Like This Picture (Game #1), most (if not all) of the players are holding a picture. If you have not played that game before this one, pass pictures of different items to each player. All the players show their pictures for about five minutes and then hold them so the rest of the group can't see them. One player starts the game by putting her own picture down and "wishing" for one of the other cards. At this point, whoever has the card she wished for has to give it to her. After that, the player who gave up his card expresses his own wish and is given the card he desires.

Example: "My hand is empty, I wish for the picture with the sun."

Variation: All players turn over their pictures so everyone can see them. If a player expresses a wish, he or she must also give the name of the person who is holding that picture.

Follow-up Games
4: Evil Fairy's Hat   ◆   26: The Seat on My Right is Empty (with a Twist)

Follow-up Games from *101 More Life Skills Games for Children*
13: Missing Person   ◆   68: Birthday Party   ◆   34: Picture Present

Evil Fairy's Hat

Props: Assorted pictures from magazines (enough for all players), a hat

Goals
- Expressing dislikes
- Finding commonalities

How to Play: From the collection of pictures (see I Like This Picture, Game #1), every player takes one that means something negative for him. The players give reasons for their choices and then, saying "I'm going to throw it into the evil fairy's hat," they toss their picture into a hat in the middle of the room.

Example: "I don't like the umbrella because it reminds me of rainy weather."

Follow-up Games
2: The Run-to Game   ◆   5: Good Fairy

Follow-up Game from *101 More Life Skills Games for Children*
17: The "I" Museum

Good Fairy

Props: Assorted pictures from magazines (enough for all players)

Goals
- Learning to avoid stereotypes
- Emphasizing the positive
- Expressing dislikes
- Learning to accept change

How to Play: All players draw a picture from the "evil fairy's hat" (see Evil Fairy's Hat, Game #4). Each player tries to recall the negative reason the card was thrown into the hat in the last game and then comes up with a positive statement to counter the negative one. If the players are having difficulty remembering the negative reason why a photo was tossed into the evil fairy's hat in the previous game, the student who threw it in the hat can state the negative reason and then allow the current player to counter with a positive statement about the item.

Example: "The picture of the umbrella was thrown into the hat because it reminded someone of bad weather, but we can have a cozy chat under the umbrella."

Follow-up Games
7: Guess What I Can Do   ◆   56: Information Please   ◆   86: Frozen Music

I Can, I Can't

Goals
- Improving self-esteem
- Seeing room for self-improvement
- Developing honesty
- Avoiding false modesty
- Developing empathy for the disabilities of others
- Learning to trust the group

How to Play: All players introduce themselves, sharing something they are good at and something they are not.

Example: "My name is Philip. I can draw well, but I'm not so good at math."

Note: This game can help children to have a more balanced view of themselves. There will be players who only want to say something positive or something negative about themselves, but this is one rule that shouldn't be broken. And remember, everybody's better at some things than others.

Reflections
- Which statement was easier for you—*I can* or *I can't*?
- Do you think you are self-confident?
- Do you know someone who is very self-confident?
- How do you become self-confident?
- How can you get better at something?

Follow-up Games
7: Guess What I Can Do ◆ 27–32: Understanding You ◆ 33–40: Working with You ◆ 45–51: Cooperation Games ◆ 52–56: Integrating New Classmates ◆ 57–70: Helping Games ◆ 95: Fairytale Surprises

Follow-up Games from *101 More Life Skills Games for Children*
13–21: How I Am ◆ 35–39: Perceiving You ◆ 53: Are You Like Me? ◆ 60–66: Integration Games ◆ 75: President of Praise

Guess What I Can Do

Goals

- Improving social awareness
- Improving visual awareness
- Developing self-esteem
- Avoiding false modesty

How to Play: A player mimes what he or she can do well. Whoever guesses what it is goes next.

Example: If a student thinks she's good at making funny faces, she keeps doing it until another player says, "Making faces!"

Reflection: Do you find it easier to express yourself with words or in pantomime?

Follow-up Games

6: I Can, I Can't ◆ 8: Observing the Room ◆ 20–40: You-Games ◆
78: Peace Language ◆ 97–101: Pantomime Play

Follow-up Games from *101 More Life Skills Games for Children*

13–21: How I Am ◆ 35–39: Perceiving You ◆ 60–66: Integration
Games ◆ 80: Face-off

Observing
the Room

Goals
- Sharpening the senses
- Learning group solidarity
- Valuing self-awareness
- Appreciating change

How to Play: The group leader says, in her own words: "Not all people notice the same things when they enter a room. Some notice the noise level, the quietness, or a particular sound; others notice the smell, the temperature, other people, or things in the room. Some people focus on just one thing, other people might see many different things."

Now the group leader asks the players to close their eyes for a minute. After they open their eyes, players take turns talking about something they noticed when their eyes were closed.

Players who mention something they don't like about the room are asked what could be changed to make them feel better. If the changes are reasonable, the group leader might consider making them as soon as possible.

Note: Distractions in the room frequently interfere with work and play. We notice this especially with newcomers and latecomers—before they can concentrate on the other players or the discussion, they must first "take in" the room.

Reflections
- What is unknown to you in this room?
- What makes the room comfortable for you?
- What other rooms does it remind you of?
- What things could be done in this room?

Role Plays
- The king's daughter in the new castle.

- The family is considering moving into a new apartment or home. What do the family members not like now; what should be different in the future?

Follow-up Games
1–5: What I Like ◆ 9: The Room's ABCs ◆ 10: Changing the Room

Follow-up Games from *101 More Life Skills Games for Children*
1–10: What I'm Feeling ◆ 33: Favorite Place ◆ 56: Designing a Classroom ◆ 60–66: Integration Games ◆ 67–73: Relationship Games ◆ 78: Jostle

The Room's ABCs

Props: Cards or other items with single letters of the alphabet written on them

Goals
- Improving visual perception
- Establishing a relationship with the room

How to Play: The group leader randomly hands out letters of the alphabet to the group, using handwritten cards or a set of carved wooden letters. The players write down objects in the room that start with the letter they have received.

Variations
- The game can be played as a scavenger hunt. In this version, players trade sheets with each other after they have written their lists and then try to find the objects on the new sheets they have received.

- Players write down their first name vertically. After every letter, they write down the objects of the room which start with that letter.

Example: "Ben"
   B blackboard, ball, book
   E eraser, elbow, edge
   N notebook, nail, number

Note: Carved wooden letters are nice, and card stock lasts longer than sheets of paper, but sheets of paper are good too because they can be nicely decorated by the players and hung up in the classroom.

Follow-up Games
8: Observing the Room ◆ 10: Changing the Room

Follow-up Games from *101 More Life Skills Games for Children*
33: Favorite Place ◆ 39: Two Peas in a Pod ◆ 85–90: Statue and Sculpting Games

Changing the Room

Goals
- Enhancing creativity
- Improving visual perception
- Developing a relationship to the group room
- Developing flexibility

How to Play: One player leaves the room, and the others change something about the room. When the missing player returns, she has to figure out what's different.

Reflections
- What makes it difficult to change many things in this room?
- When have you noticed something unusual in a place you go to often?
- How much do unusual things scare you?

Role Plays
- The children acting as parents tell other "adults" how their apartment looked after they left their children home alone.
- An avant-garde interior designer suggests some crazy things.
- Newlyweds enter their new apartment and discover their friends have pulled a trick on them—like rearranging the furniture or filling a room with balloons.

Follow-up Games
5: Good Fairy ◆ 8: Observing the Room ◆ 11: What's Made of This? ◆ 28: You Sculpt Me ◆ 68: Moving Help ◆ 84–92: Statue and Sculpting Games

Follow-up Games from *101 More Life Skills Games for Children*
33: Favorite Place ◆ 40: The Incredible Two-Handed Pen ◆ 85–90: Statue and Sculpting Games

What's Made of This?

Goals
- Developing tactile awareness
- Improving visual perception
- Developing ability to form pairs and work as a team
- Making contact

How to Play: The group chooses a material, like wood or plastic or glass. Players walk around the room, touching as many objects made out of that material as possible. Touching could mean tapping, stroking, taking into one's hands, pressing, or knocking on it. Then, in turns, each player names a different object made of the material.

Variations
- Where is there water in this room? (This variation requires good observation skills.)
- Touch any soft/small/smooth/round objects!
- Sitting in a circle, name pairs of opposites: the wall is rough, the window is smooth, etc.
- A "run-to" game: A player names a quality, for example, "round." Every player runs to a round object in the room. There can be more than one person at one object (see The Run-to Game, Game #2).
- Draw a picture or a doodle with the following titles: "round," "pointed," "water," "wood."

Reflections
- Which materials, forms, colors, and surfaces do you like?

Follow-up Games
12: The Traveling Mystery ◆ 17: Telling Sounds Apart ◆
27–32: Understanding You ◆ 39: Twins ◆ 57–70: Helping Games ◆

87: Statue Pairs ◆ 93: Bad News and Good News Pairs ◆
94: Fairytale Personalities

Follow-up Games from *101 More Life Skills Games for Children*
5: Moodles ◆ 20: Pieces of Personality ◆ 21: Help Wanted ◆
35–39: Perceiving You ◆ 53: Are You Like Me? ◆ 54: We Are Alike

What I Observe

The Traveling Mystery

Props: Various objects to be passed around

Goals
- Developing tactile awareness
- Calming down
- Improving concentration

How to Play: The group leader and the players sit in a circle facing inward. Behind his back, the group leader hands different objects one by one to the player sitting to his left. The mystery object "travels" around the circle as each player passes it to the next player behind her back without looking at it. Before passing an object on, a player whispers into the ear of the person on his right (the person who passed them the object) what kind of object he thinks it is.

Examples
- Unopened can of water
- Small building blocks
- Three marbles

Variations
- Geometrical shapes, wooden letters
- Perfume bottles

Note: Passing objects around a circle is a simple way of making a connection. Players not only make contact with their neighbors, they also carefully watch the players sitting opposite them: their facial expressions, how skillful or clumsy they are. These "silence exercises" tend to calm the group down and help them focus.

Follow-up Games
13: A Piece at a Time ◆ 20: Traveling Names ◆ 33–40: Working with

You ♦ 41–44: Warming-up Games for the Group ♦ 45–51: Cooperation Games ♦ 78: Peace Language ♦ 82: Vampire ♦ 97–101: Pantomime Play

Follow-up Games from *101 More Life Skills Games for Children*
11: Brainstorm ♦ 25: Zip Zap Names ♦ 40–45: Working with You ♦ 47: Name Chain ♦ 51: The Goofy Game ♦ 52–59: Cooperation Games

A Piece at a Time

Props: A puzzle with a very small number of pieces

Goals
- Improving visual perception
- Making contact
- Calming down
- Developing concentration

How to Play: The game leader passes around the pieces of a puzzle one by one. The players look at the pieces and silently pass them on until everyone has seen them all. All the players say what they think the puzzle will look like when it's put together. Then it's put together in the center of the circle, and we see who got it right.

Variations
- The group leader puts several finished puzzles on the floor in addition to the one that was circulated. The players guess which puzzle was circulated.
- After one puzzle has circulated, put several pieces from different puzzles on the floor. Which ones belong to the puzzle that was circulated?

Reflection: In order to be able to put the pieces together, some players say they remember words that remind them of each puzzle piece; others try to remember the shape of the piece; others try to "take a picture" of the individual images in their minds. How did you do it?

Follow-up Games
8–19: What I Observe ◆ 27–32: Understanding You ◆ 76: Detective
◆ 97–101: Pantomime Play

Follow-up Game from *101 More Life Skills Games for Children*
32: See How You Are

Seeing with Your Ears

Props: A rubber ball

Goals
- Improving acoustic perception
- Recognizing differences in how people perceive sounds

How to Play: The group leader drops a solid rubber ball. One half of the group closes their eyes and guesses how high the ball is bouncing by the sound it makes. They mark the height with their hands. When they don't hear anything any more, they point to the place where they heard the last sound coming from. The observing half of the group reflects about what they observed.

Reflection: Which differences in perception do the hands of the players show us? This game reminds us that we can't always trust the senses.

Follow-up Games
8–19: What I Observe ◆ 27–32: Understanding You ◆ 61: Cry for Help ◆ 67: Crocodile Tears ◆ 75: Polite Wild Animals ◆ 79: Rumors

What I Observe

Telling Noises Apart

Props: Ten objects you can make noises with

Goals
- Improving acoustic perception
- Developing acoustic memory
- Understanding how we learn

How to Play: The group leader places up to ten objects in the center of the group circle. The players close their eyes. The leader makes noises with up to six of the objects. The players then open their eyes and try to guess which objects were used to make these noises.

Reflections
- Not everything you hear can be easily identified. Also, you can't remember everything you hear. What do perceiving, remembering, and learning depend on?
- Can we get better at this game if we practice?

Role Plays
- A witness tells the police what sounds he had heard at the scene of the crime. The police then try to figure out what happened based on the sounds described.
- Improvisation with noises: "Haunted Castle"

Follow-up Games
14: Seeing with Your Ears and all of its suggested follow-up games ◆
17: Telling Sounds Apart

Stand Up for Your Instrument

Props: A number of percussion and/or Orff instruments

Goals
- Improving acoustic perception
- Fostering self-evaluation

How to Play: In the middle of the circle are several percussion and/or Orff instruments, such as bongos, tambourines, triangles, shakers, and metallophones. All players in the circle name an instrument whose sound they like or think they are going to like. Then they try out all the instruments one by one. If a player likes the sound of an instrument, he or she stands up.

Reflection: If you weren't already familiar with an instrument, did the actual sound differ from how you thought it was going to sound?

Follow-up Games
1–5: What I Like ◆ 15: Telling Noises Apart ◆ 17: Telling Sounds Apart ◆ 27–32: Understanding You

Follow-up Games from *101 More Life Skills Games for Children*
1–10: What I'm Feeling ◆ 13–21: How I Am ◆ 34: Picture Present

Telling Sounds Apart

Props: Percussion and/or Orff instruments for all players except one; a blackboard or easel pad on which to write

Goals
- Improving acoustic perception
- Identifying acoustic qualities
- Reducing aggression
- Warming-up to the group

How to Play: The following qualities are written on the blackboard: loud, quiet, bright, dark, metallic, rhythmic, soft, aggressive.

All players but one have an instrument. They are facing the board. The player without an instrument has his or her back against the board. The group leader points to one of the qualities, and the players respond accordingly using their instruments. After half a minute the player without an instrument guesses which quality they meant.

Reflection: Which quality did you like to play best?

Follow-up Games
1–5: What I Like ◆ 11: What's Made of This? ◆ 18: Collecting Sound Qualities ◆ 94: Fairytale Personalities ◆ 97–101: Pantomime Play

Follow-up Games from *101 More Life Skills Games for Children*
8: Mood Music ◆ 13–21: How I Am

What I Observe

Collecting
Sound Qualities

Props: Percussion and/or Orff instruments for half of the players; paper and pens/pencils for writing

Goals
- Improving acoustic perception
- Identifying acoustic qualities
- Making contact
- Enhancing creativity

How to Play: Half of the group members have instruments. Each player thinks about what quality he or she wants to express on his or her instrument. They write this quality on several slips of paper. Now all players simultaneously play their qualities. The players without instruments go from one musician to the next and try to guess what quality they are playing. If they guess right, they get a paper slip with the quality written on it. After the players without instruments have finished making their guesses, they trade roles with the players with instruments and play the game again.

Examples

- Wild
- Soft
- Rhythmical
- Loud

Follow-up Games

17: Telling Sounds Apart and all of its suggested follow-up games ◆
19: Song Memory

Song Memory

Props: Percussion and/or Orff instruments for all players except one

Goals
- Developing partnership
- Learning to form groups
- Improving acoustic perception
- Making contact
- Enhancing creativity

How to Play: One person is chosen as the guesser and leaves the room. The other players pair up and choose a song or nursery rhyme and start humming it together. Each pair continues humming the same song as they separate and walk into different parts of the room. The guessing person returns and tries to put the pairs back together.

Reflections
- How did you become a pair?
- Who had to adapt to his partner?

Variation: Form larger groups of four or even eight.

Follow-up Games
18: Collecting Sound Qualities ◆ 27–32: Understanding You ◆ 33–40: Working with You ◆ 45–51: Cooperation Games ◆ 53: The Grouping Game ◆ 77: Frontline ◆ 87: Statue Pairs ◆ 93: Bad News and Good News Pairs

Follow-up Games from *101 More Life Skills Games for Children*
8: Mood Music ◆ 40–45: Working with You ◆ 52–59: Cooperation Games ◆ 79: War Dance

You Games

Getting to Know You
Games 20–26

Understanding You
Games 27–32

Working with You
Games 33–40

Traveling Names

Goals
- Getting acquainted
- Making contact
- Winning trust
- Dealing with secrets

How to Play: Sitting in the circle, the group leader whispers the name of one group member into the ear of the person sitting to her left. In the same way, the name is passed around the circle until it reaches its owner. When it does, that player says his own name aloud. Now it's his or her turn to send a different name on a trip around the circle.

Note: In this game, the whispered word must not be garbled, as happens in the game "Telephone." If you didn't hear clearly, have the word repeated. Children love mysteries and secrets, and there is something mysterious and intimate about whispering into somebody's ear.

Reflections
- In this game, a secret is being passed on. Is it still a secret if it is passed on?
- What does it feel like to wait for a secret to reach you?

- Have you ever passed on a secret you were asked to keep?
- Have you ever trusted someone to keep a secret and they shared that secret with someone else you didn't want to hear about it? How did that make you feel?

Follow-up Games

1–5: I-Games ◆ 21: Crossword Puzzle Names ◆ 41–44: Warming-up Games for the Group ◆ 52–56: Integrating New Classmates

Follow-up Games from *101 More Life Skills Games for Children*

22–34: Getting to Know You ◆ 29: Disposable Secrets ◆
46–51: Warming-up Games for the Group ◆ 63: The Blind Group ◆ 64: Blind Pool

Crossword Puzzle Names

Props: Paper and pens/pencils for writing

Goals
- Getting acquainted
- Making contact

How to Play: Every player writes down his name in capital letters on a piece of paper. Now he looks for players whose names can be added to it, like in a crossword puzzle.

Example: Maria

```
        J   L
    T H O M A S
        S   T
        E R I C A
            S
            H   M
        M A R I A
            N   D
        A H M A D   M
                V A N E S S A
            G I N   I
                D
```

Follow-up Games
20: Traveling Names and all of its suggested follow-up games ◆
22: Gathering Names

Gathering Names

Props: Paper and pencils, pens, crayons, and markers for writing and drawing

Goals
- Getting acquainted
- Making contact

How to Play: Every player writes his name on a regular sheet of paper in a creative way. Then every player asks as many players as possible to add their names to the paper.

Examples
- In colorful letters
- In rainbow colors
- Tiny, huge
- In bold
- In chaotic type

Follow-up Games
21: Crossword Puzzle Names and all of its suggested follow-up games ◆
23: Autograph Book

Autograph Book

Props: Paper and pens (perhaps with different color inks)

Goals
- Getting acquainted
- Making contact
- Remembering names

How to Play: This game is designed to be played by children who do not yet know each other. Every player has a sheet of paper and a pen, possibly in different colors. All players walk around and ask up to six players for an autograph. They need to try to remember the faces that go along with the autographs, because once they have all six autographs, they then need to find two of the six whose names they remember. Once every player has found two people, they each take turns introducing their two players to the rest of the group.

Follow-up Games
22: Gathering Names ◆ 24: Building Names

Building Names

Props: Paper and pens/pencils for writing

Goals
- Learning names
- Learning how to spell group members' names
- Fostering initial contact

How to Play: All the players write their names in capital letters on a small piece of paper. Underneath, each player adds as many blanks for writing as his name has letters. He then passes it on to the person sitting on his left. She writes the first letter of his name in the first blank and passes the piece of paper on. Her neighbor writes the second letter in the second blank, and so on. The piece of paper is passed on until the name is finished. The player who puts in the last letter then hands the paper back to the person whose name is written on it.

Follow-up Games
23: Autograph Book and all of its suggested follow-up games ◆
25: Mirror Names

Mirror Names

Props: Tracing paper; pens/pencils for writing; tape

Goals
- Fostering contact
- Getting acquainted

How to Play: The game is ideal for children who do not yet know each other. All players write their names in capital letters on tracing paper. Then they ask the other players to tape it to their backs in reverse so the name appears in mirror writing. All players walk around and meet one another, giving each other a friendly tap on the back and greeting each other by name.

Variation: For groups in which everybody already knows everybody else's name, the players can choose nicknames or pseudonyms—say, the name of a celebrity—instead.

Follow-up Games
26: The Seat on My Right Is Empty (with a Twist) ◆ 24: Building Names and all of its suggested follow-up games

26

any size

Getting to Know You

The Seat on My Right Is Empty (with a Twist)

Props: Chairs for all players plus one additional chair

Goals
- Fostering contact
- Getting acquainted
- Trying out forms of requests
- Improving integration into the group

How to Play: There is one chair too many in the circle. The person sitting to the left of the empty chair says, "The seat on my right is empty. I'd like

The seat on my right is empty

101 Life Skills Games for Children **47**

Jake to sit here." Jake sits down, leaving his own chair empty. The person sitting to the left of that chair asks another person to sit there.

Variation: In this version, players ask for a new neighbor in different ways: begging, bossily, sadly, eagerly.

Examples
- "It would be so nice if you, Lisa, sat next to me...please!"
- "Lisa, come here immediately!"

Follow-up Games
1–5: What I Like ◆ 20–40: You Games ◆ 41–44: Warming-up Games for the Group ◆ 45–51: Cooperation Games ◆ 52–56: Integrating New Classmates ◆ 63: I Fell in the Well ◆ 65: Brother, Help! Sister, Help!

Follow-up Games from *101 More Life Skills Games for Children*
20: Pieces of Personality ◆ 22–45: You Games ◆ 46–51: Warming-up Games for the Group ◆ 52–59: Cooperation Games ◆ 64: Blind Pool ◆ 67–73: Relationship Games

I Met My Match

Props: Paper and pens/pencils for writing

Goals
- Forming relationships
- Discovering similarities

How to Play: Each player takes a sheet of paper and draws on it the outline of his hands and feet, then adds his name. Then all the papers are laid on the floor. Each player whose hand or foot size matches one on the floor adds her name inside the drawing it matches.

Note: This game highlights physical differences and therefore might not be appropriate for certain groups of players.

Follow-up Games
1–5: What I Like ◆ 28: You Sculpt Me ◆ 33–40: Working with You ◆ 50: Tug of War

28

Understanding You

You
Sculpt Me

Goals
- Reducing fear of physical contact
- Building trust in a partner
- Interacting with sensitivity
- Improving communication
- Dealing with aggression

How to Play: In this partner exercise, one player is a sculptor, the other one is the clay to be sculpted. The sculptor sculpts the clay into a person, a plant, an animal, or an object. This is a silent game, since clay cannot speak. At the end, the clay tries to guess what he or she has been sculpted into.

Variations
- The players change roles. Now the clay tries to build the exact same sculpture.
- The sculptor is commissioned by the group leader or his or her partner to build something specific like a snowman, a scarecrow, a knight, a pop star, or a mannequin.

Role Play: The stubborn sculpture keeps ruining the design.

Follow-up Games
27: I Met My Match ◆ 29: You Reflect Me ◆ 33–40: Working with You ◆ 45–51: Cooperation Games ◆ 57–70: Helping Games ◆ 71: Animals in the Jungle ◆ 84–92: Statue and Sculpting Games

Follow-up Games from *101 More Life Skills Games for Children*
40–45: Working with You ◆ 85–90: Statue and Sculpting Games ◆ 94: Shadow Play

You Reflect Me

Props: Background music (optional)

Goals
- Developing sensitivity
- Developing partnership
- Improving visual perception
- Improving communication

How to Play: Two players stand about three feet apart from each other. One player starts moving to soft music with small, slow arm movements. The player opposite joins in and imitates the movements as if he or she was a mirror. Now they add their legs. Both players crouch or sit without taking their eyes off each other. Now they switch, and the "reflection" makes movements that are imitated by her partner.

Variations
- The players move sideways or backwards in the opposite directions of one another (i.e., if one player moves right, the other moves left).
- One player directs a whole group.

Note: In order for the game to be successful, slow-motion movements are essential; otherwise the partner cannot keep up.

Reflections
- What was more fun—to be a leader or a follower?
- What happens if you don't agree on who is going to be the leader?

Follow-up Games
28: You Sculpt Me and all of its suggested follow-up games ◆ 30: You Draw Me

Understanding You

You
Draw Me

Props: Paper and pens/pencils for drawing

Goals
- Improving visual awareness
- Making contact
- Forming pairs
- Learning to observe

How to Play: The group is divided into pairs. Two players stand or sit opposite each other with paper and pencil. They draw each other without looking at the paper. When they're finished, they write down the name of their partner. Now they hang up all portraits and enjoy looking at them.

Reflections
- Did you feel awkward when your partner looked at you so closely?
- When you were drawing, did you notice something about your partner that you would have overlooked if you hadn't looked so closely?

Follow-up Games
7: Guess What I Can Do ◆ 29: You Reflect Me ◆ 31: You Move Me

Understanding You

You Move Me

Props: Chairs for half of the group; background music (optional)

Goals
- Developing trust
- Developing sensitive behavior

How to Play: The group is divided into partners. One player sits on a chair, and her partner stands in front of her holding her by the wrists. To music playing in the background, the standing partners symmetrically move their partners' arms. The sitting partners try to experience the movements in different ways: with open eyes, with closed eyes, with loose arms, with stiff arms, with heavy arms, with light arms, with resistance, without resistance.

After some time, the players switch places.

Note: This game requires a lot of trust. It should be preceded by warm-up games, and the group leader should make sure that only players who get along well become partners.

Follow-up Games
8–19: What I Observe ◆ 28: You Sculpt Me and all of its suggested follow-up games ◆ 30: You Draw Me ◆ 32: When It Rains, It Pours ◆ 33–40: Working with You

When It Rains, It Pours

Goals

- Developing tactile perception
- Developing sensitivity
- Developing trust with a partner
- Relaxing

How to Play: One player holds out his hand. Using his fingers, his partner creates various weather effects on his partner's hand to simulate a storm: drizzle, rain drops, downpour, snowfall, snowstorm, hail. After a while, the sun comes out and the thunderstorm stops. The partners switch.

Variation: The touches follow the beat of music.

Note: For this game, quite a lot of trust is required of both partners. If both players have experience with this kind of game, they don't necessarily have to know each other well.

Reflection: Did your partner touch you roughly or gently? Which touches felt good and which didn't?

Follow-up Games

11: What's Made of This? ◆ 12: The Traveling Mystery ◆ 31: You Move Me ◆ 33–40: Working with You ◆ 45: Together on One Chair ◆ 52: Wake Up! ◆ 57–70: Helping Games ◆ 71: Animals in the Jungle ◆ 82: Vampire ◆ 91: Acting Out Pictures

Follow-up Games from *101 More Life Skills Games for Children*

40–45: Working with You ◆ 64: Blind Pool

Holding Me with Your Eyes

Goals
- Keeping eye contact
- Developing partnership
- Being considerate

How to Play: The players separate into pairs and then everyone walks around the room, each person walking at least four yards from their partner. No matter how much the other pairs distract them, they never lose eye contact with their partner.

Variation: Every now and then, the group leader says, "Close your eyes and find each other." The players walk towards each other with eyes closed, either silently or by shouting to help each other (depending on what had been agreed on).

Follow-up Games
19: Song Memory ◆ 27–32: Understanding You ◆ 34: Helping Hands ◆ 41–44: Warming-up Games for the Group ◆ 57–70: Helping Games

Helping Hands

Props: Paper and pens/pencils for writing

Goals
- Learning to cooperate
- Learning to coordinate
- Being dependent on a partner

How to Play: Each player thinks of an activity that usually needs two hands and writes it down in a short sentence. It must be an activity that can be done in the room.

Now the slips of paper get shuffled, and players pair off. Every pair draws one slip from the pile. All partners put one hand behind their backs, leaving the other hand free. Now they perform the task written on the paper with their free hands working together. Then another task is chosen for all the partners to try.

Examples
- Take the cap off a bottle
- Tie and untie a shoelace
- Dry a dish
- Wash hands with soap
- Clap hands

Follow-up Games
33: Holding Me with Your Eyes and all of its suggested follow-up games
◆ 35: Picking Up Sticks Together ◆ 45–51: Cooperation Games

Picking Up Sticks Together

Props: Paper and pens/pencils for writing

Goals
- Learning to cooperate
- Learning to coordinate while doing something fast
- Experiencing dependency

How to Play: The group leader distributes a large number of popsicle sticks or similar objects around the room. The players form pairs and take each other by the hand. At a signal, the pairs collect as many sticks as possible without letting go of each other's hands.

Reflection: How were the winners able to collect the most sticks?

Follow-up Games
All suggested follow-up games for 33: Holding Me with Your Eyes ◆
34: Helping Hands ◆ 36: New World Record

New World Record

Goals
- Learning to cooperate
- Learning to coordinate

How to Play: The players get together in pairs. Each pair has 20 minutes to set a record and tell the group about it. The accomplishment can be simple or bizarre.

Examples
- Throwing and catching a ball
- Playing Frisbee without dropping it
- Non-stop leapfrog
- Wheelbarrow long-distance record
- The highest building-block tower

Note: This game is about accomplishments that cannot be achieved by one player alone. It's not about comparison and competition with other pairs. The more varied and creative the record attempts are, the less likely it is that pairs will start competing with each other.

Follow-up Games
All suggested follow-up games for 33: Holding Me with Your Eyes ◆
37: Dance Partners ◆ 35: Picking Up Sticks Together ◆
45–51: Cooperation Games

Dance Partners

Props: Background music (optional)

Goals
- Learning to cooperate
- Leading and following
- Developing consideration for others
- Developing trust
- Experiencing music
- Experiencing closeness and distance
- Warming up

How to Play: As in You Reflect Me (Game #29), partners try to imitate each other's movements. In this game, however, the dancers don't decide in advance who determines the moves. The way they move should change frequently; each partner has to become attuned to the other's movements.

Variation: One player is the dancer and the other one is the musician, who adapts her playing to match the dancing movements of her partner. When there are several dancers, they should try to coordinate their dancing and the musicians should coordinate their playing as well.

Follow-up Games
36: New World Record ◆ 38: Patty-Cake ◆ 41–44: Warming-up Games for the Group ◆ 45–51: Cooperation Games ◆ 57–70: Helping Games ◆ 72: Tug of War II

Follow-up Games from *101 More Life Skills Games for Children*
22–34: Getting to Know You ◆ 40–45: Working with You ◆ 46–51: Warming-up Games for the Group ◆ 52–59: Cooperation Games ◆ 60–66: Integration Games

Working with You

Patty-Cake

Goals
- Learning to cooperate
- Accomplishing a task
- Enhancing creativity
- Learning to coordinate

How to Play: Two players are sitting on chairs opposite each other. They recite a rhyme they both know, like "Mary Had a Little Lamb."

While reciting the rhyme, with each beat, players alternately clap their hands and slap their thighs, clap hands, slap thighs, and so forth. Both players try to do this exercise simultaneously. Next comes clapping with their partners

They slap their own thighs, and then clap the hands of their partners, then their own hands, then slap their own thighs again, and so forth. The players change partners several times in order to have different experiences. With the new partners, they could also invent new clapping variations, or have their new partners show them other variations. The players try new clapping variations by clapping their right hands and left hands together alternately.

Variation: Invent nonsense rhymes and clap to them.

Reflections
- Which partner was it easier to clap with?
- What kind of rhyme was most fun for you?

Follow-up Games
37: Dance Partners and all of its suggested follow-up games ◆
39: Twins

Working with You

Twins

Goals
- Learning to cooperate
- Improving visual perception
- Improving social awareness
- Developing partnership

How to Play: One or several players leave the room for a few minutes. The other players form pairs of twins. They try to find a partner who most resembles them or, even if they don't look like someone else to begin with, they can manipulate their appearance so that they have things in common with another player. Swapping sweaters or jackets might help. Now all players walk around the room. The players that were sent out are called back into the room and are asked to guess who the twins are. Twins that are identified come together and hold hands.

Examples
- Both twins have one trouser leg rolled up.
- Both twins keep their hands in their pockets.

Follow-up Games

40: Fair Ball ◆ 38: Patty-Cake ◆ 31–44: Warming-up Games for the Group ◆ 45–51: Cooperation Games ◆ 76: The Detective ◆ 78: Language of Peace ◆ 84–92: Statue and Sculpting Games ◆ 97–101: Pantomime Play

Follow-up Games from *101 More Life Skills Games for Children*

35–39: Perceiving You ◆ 40–45: Working with You ◆ 52–59: Cooperation Games ◆ 80: Face-off

groups
of 3

Working with You

Fair Ball

Props: Balls, Frisbees, etc., for playing catch

Goals

- Learning to cooperate
- Performing
- Developing tolerance
- Forming partnerships
- Being fair and just

How to Play: Two players stand across from each other, several yards apart, and play catch—trying not to drop whatever they're throwing (ball, Frisbee...). A referee awards them two points for every good throw. Likewise, two points for every good catch. If the throw is bad but the other player makes the catch anyway, he or she gets three points. If the catcher tries hard to make a catch but misses, he gets a point for effort.

Reflections

- How could the rules of the game be made harder or easier?
- Is it always more fun if the rules are easier?
- Were you happy with the referee?
- What would the game be like without a referee?

- Can you think of any situations in everyday life in which it helps to have a referee?

Role Plays
- The unfair referee
- My siblings always get favored!

Follow-up Games
45–51: Cooperation Games

We Games

Warming-up Games for the Group
Games 41–44

Cooperation Games
Games 45–51

Integrating New Classmates
Games 52–56

Helping Games
Games 57–70

Aggression Games
Games 71–83

Balloon Dance

Props: Balloons for all players; pens or markers for writing on the balloons; music

Goals
- Warming up and relaxing
- Learning names
- Reducing inhibitions
- Making contact
- Animating the group

How to Play: Every player blows up a balloon, draws a simple self-portrait on it, and then writes her name on it. When the music starts, the players let their balloons dance above their heads. Together, while dancing, everyone helps to keep the balloons from touching the floor. When the music stops, everyone catches one at random, and tries to find its owner. Once all balloons are back with their owners, the balloon dance starts again.

Variations
- The same game as above, but in small groups, organized by the colors of the balloons.
- In small groups, organized by the number of letters contained in first names (e.g., group A: three to five letters; group B: six or more letters).

Note: In this game, all players introduce themselves to each other through the self-portraits they draw on their balloons. The drawing and dancing is relaxing, and it makes the first contact easier. Balloons and light music also contribute to feeling at ease, and funny self-portraits provide amusement. Every player is engaged and must make contact with other players. These factors help children overcome their shyness.

Follow-up Games
41–44: Warming-up Games for the Group

That Seat's Taken

Props: Chairs for all players except one

Goals
- Warming up and relaxation
- Animating the group
- Discovering similarities
- Being considerate

How to Play: The circle of chairs is missing one. The leader chooses one player to stand in the middle of the circle. That player then names a characteristic that several players share, like blond hair. All players with this

characteristic have to quickly get out of their seats and try to find another one to sit in. The player in the center also tries to get a seat. Whoever ends up without a seat gets to call out the next characteristic.

Examples
- Wearing blue jeans
- Brown eyes
- Born in winter
- A girl

Notes
- This game may potentially emphasize physical differences. If doing so is not appropriate for the group, the leader should steer the class to name nonphysical characteristics.
- Players may also accidentally bump into each other in this game, so if that might be a problem in any way, you may want to modify or skip this game.

Follow-up Games
41–44: Warming-up Games for the Group

Warming-up Games
for the Group

Greeting Game

Goals
- Warming up
- Making first contact
- Reducing inhibitions

How to Play: The game is perfect for children who do no yet know each other. The players walk around the room. Music plays in the background. Every time the music stops (for approximately half a minute), the group leader gives a command that the players must carry out.

Examples
- "Ask the name of the person closest to you!"
- "Shake as many hands as possible!"
- "Tap as many players as possible on their shoulders!"
- "Ask as many players as possible for their names!"

Notes
- The use of music in this game reduces any tension and relaxes the group.
- It is important to point out before the game that anyone who touches another player roughly will not be allowed to keep playing.

Follow-up Games
41–44: Warming-up Games for the Group

Good Morning!

Goals
- Warming up
- Initiating first contact
- Reducing inhibitions
- Experimenting with behavior
- Developing everyday manners
- Expressing moods

How to Play: As in Greeting Game (Game #43), the players walk around the room as relaxing music plays in the background. In this game, though, every time the music stops, the group leader announces a new "walking assignment."

Examples
- It's early in the morning. You haven't had enough sleep, so trudge along without looking at the people you encounter.
- Today you are well rested and in a good mood, so smile at everyone as you stroll to school.
- You're in a good mood but also in a hurry. Rush to school and greet the people you meet with a friendly and quick "Hello" or "Good morning!"
- Your school hall is packed with people. While you try to press through the crowd, you see friends on the other side of the room and wave to them, shout hello, or call attention to yourself in some other way.
- Today you have no school. You have time to say hello to people, say a few nice words, and then move on.

Reflections
- Do any of the behaviors demonstrated remind you of ways you sometimes act?
- Which behavior of other people do you like?
- What do adults consider "good behavior"?

Role Plays
- Hey you, don't you know how to say hello?
- A conflict on the way to school

Follow-up Games
41–44: Warming-up Games for the Group ◆ 52: Wake Up!

Follow-up Games from *101 More Life Skills Games for Children*
1–10: What I'm Feeling

Together on One Chair

Props: Chairs for all players except one

Goals
- Learning to cooperate
- Building group spirit

How to Play: Make two rows of chairs with their backs to each other. There should be enough seats for all but one person.

When the group leader turns on the music, the players walk clockwise around the two rows of chairs. When the music stops, everybody tries to take a seat. Since, to begin with, there is one less chair than there are players, the player who doesn't get a seat has to share one with someone else (only two players are allowed on one chair). Each time the music stops, the group leader removes a chair so that more and more players are forced to take a seat next to somebody else. When all of the chairs eventually have two players on them, children without a chair have to hold hands with a seated player. In the end, there is only one chair left, two players are on it, and everybody else is holding one of the seated players' hands.

Variation: How many players can sit on one chair without touching the floor?

Reflections
- Did you try to sit on a chair all the time, or did you not mind holding someone's hand?
- Did you care who you shared a chair with, or did you choose a specific person? Were you rejected, or were you accepted without problems?
- Did you encourage anyone to share your chair or hold your hand?
- How do you feel when it's crowded?

Notes
- This game is not designed as an introduction for completely new

groups, but it can be played as a warming-up game with game-experienced groups or groups whose members know each other well.

- If the physical contact that will likely occur in this game might be a problem in your group or setting, you may want to modify or skip this game.

Role Plays
- Crowded train department
- My seat in class is occupied today

Follow-up Games
33–40: Working with You ◆ 46: Take a Bow ◆ 57–70: Helping Games ◆ 90: Class Picture

Follow-up Games from *101 More Life Skills Games for Children*
40–45: Working with You ◆ 52–59: Cooperation Games ◆ 60–66: Integration Games ◆ 67–73: Relationship Games ◆ 74: Something Nice ◆ 85–90: Statue and Sculpting Games ◆ 91–92: Simulation Games

Cooperation Games

Take a Bow

Props: Chairs for all players

Goals
- Learning to cooperate
- Making contact
- Calming down
- Concentrating

How to Play: In this game, all the players sit in chairs arranged in a circle. One of them gets up very quietly, walks over to another, and bows. Then the second person stands up quietly and approaches a third player. The first player now sits down on the chair that the second player just got up from. This game can go on forever! No talking, coughing, banging, or giggling allowed! Any noise stops the game.

Variation: Two players approach the center of the circle simultaneously and greet each other silently as they meet. Each asks one other player to stand up. Now the two new players silently greet each other in the middle.

Note: This game can also be played as an introduction with a new group.

Role Plays
- Giving your seat to somebody on the bus.
- Letting someone cut in front of you in line.

Follow-up Games
47: Boom Box ◆ 45: Together on One Chair and all of its suggested follow-up games

Boom Box

Goals
- Learning to cooperate
- Reducing aggression

How to Play: The players listen to sound coming from an artificial sound source—a radio, a cassette recorder, or a CD of noises—and try to imitate what they hear. The volume of the machine has to be kept at a level that allows the players to respond. A conductor who indicates the desired volume by raising and lowering her hands can be helpful.

Variations
- One group is making moderate noise; the other group is trying to drown it out with similar noise.
- All players walk around. Everyone shouts something to or asks something of a person far away. Because they are all doing it simultaneously, they try to drown each other out.

Reflections
- Have you ever felt like screaming?
- Are there people who silence you by yelling?
- How well do you tolerate noise?
- Do you know anyone who doesn't tolerate noise well?
- Is shouting always a sign of aggression?

Role Plays
- The bad telephone connection.
- Grandpa is hard of hearing.

Follow-up Games
All follow-up games suggested for 45: Together on One Chair ◆
48: Beat the Clock ◆ 71–83: Aggression Games

Follow-up Games from *101 More Life Skills Games for Children*

74–84: Aggression Games

Cooperation Games

Beat
the Clock

Props: Chairs for all players

Goal
- Cooperating nonverbally

How to Play: Players sit in chairs arranged in a circle. The leader shouts a command, such as "arrange the chairs like in a movie theater!" The players immediately and silently rearrange the chairs as quickly as they can, and sit down again. With a stopwatch, the leader times them. The group can try to break its own records.

Examples
- Restaurant
- Bus
- Train
- Circus
- Office

Variation: The group leader chooses someone to be "It." That player leaves the room for ten minutes, taking with her a quiet task like homework or a good book to read. At some point during those ten minutes, but not right away, the other players quietly fulfil a command given by the group leader about how to arrange the chairs. If "It" hears any noise, she can open the door within the ten minutes, and if she sees any player not sitting in a chair, she wins. But if everyone is sitting down when the spy opens the door, whether the chairs have been rearranged or not, the group wins. If ten minutes go by and the group still hasn't rearranged the chairs, it doesn't matter how quiet they've been—they still lose, and "It" wins.

Follow-up Games
All follow-up games suggested for 45: Together on One Chair ◆
47: Boom Box ◆ 49: Building Skyscrapers

Building Skyscrapers

Props: A wide assortment of objects of various shapes and sizes

Goal
- Learning to cooperate

How to Play: The group sits in a circle around a number of objects of different shapes and sizes. Several players stay outside the circle as observers. When signaled by the group leader, the players in the circle build the highest possible sculpture they can with the objects they have been given. The players may hold the sculpture up to keep it from falling.

The game is repeated several times. At the end, the observers report their impressions to the group.

Variation: The players may not hold up the sculpture to keep it from falling.

Note: The objects could be balls, other sports equipment, or backpacks. Be careful not to include heavy or sharp objects.

Reflections
- Who is happy with what the group has accomplished?
- Who felt they contributed enough or too little?
- Did anyone feel that not enough attention was paid to him?
- Did anyone have the impression that others in the group didn't do enough?

Follow-up Games
45: Together on One Chair and all of its suggested follow-up games ◆
48: Beat the Clock ◆ 97: Getting Stronger

Cooperation Games

Tug of War

Props: Strong rope at least 10–15 feet long; cushions and/or mattresses (optional)

Goals
- Dealing with victory and defeat
- Dealing with competition appropriately
- Dealing with loss appropriately
- Praising others' accomplishments

How to Play: Every player gets a number. They sit in a wide circle on the floor. At the center is a rope. The group leader shouts two numbers. The two players called jump up, grab opposite ends of the rope and try to pull each other across a line. If a player misses his turn as a result of not paying attention, the other player automatically wins.

Variation: Blue shirts against red shirts.

Reflections
- What did you find difficult? Did you feel it was an unequal contest?
- How did the players react to doing well and not doing well?
- How did you feel after the contest?
- How could the rules be changed in order to make the fight fairer?
- What can the winners do so the other players don't get angry or feel humiliated?

Role Plays
- It's your fault that we lost the match!
- Mom, I'm not going to soccer practice!
- You only won because you played unfair!
- I'm the best!

Follow-up Games
48: Beat the Clock ◆ 49: Building Skyscrapers ◆ 51: Paper Streamer ◆ 72: Tug of War II ◆ 97: Getting Stronger

Paper Streamer

Props: A broadsheet or other newspaper

Goals
- Learning to cooperate
- Improving dexterity
- Developing tolerance
- Developing patience
- Bonding with a group

How to Play: Players sit in a circle. One player starts tearing a one-inch strip from the edge of a newspaper, stopping one inch from the bottom of the page so it hangs down. She passes it on to the person sitting to her left, and this person starts tearing in the opposite direction. In this way, a paper streamer is created. How long can it get? Measure it each time, to set a new record. The player who breaks the streamer has to start a new one.

Variation: Small groups of players attempt to tear the shape of an animal out of newspaper.

Reflections
- Do you consider yourself good at things like this?
- What are some problems you experienced playing this game?
- Do you know someone who is usually patient when a misfortune occurs?
- How can one be patient?
- Where does impatience come from?
- How does one deal with impatient people?

Note: While explaining the game and before the game starts, the group leader should discuss how to react when someone has the misfortune of tearing the streamer. After having this discussion it probably won't be necessary for you to remind the children to be patient and tolerant—they tend to police themselves.

Follow-up Games

12: The Traveling Mystery ◆ 33–40: Working with You ◆
All suggested follow-up games for 45: Together on One Chair ◆
50: Tug of War

Follow-up Games from *101 More Life Skills Games for Children*

40–45: Working with You

Wake Up!

Goals

- Reducing fear of contact
- Observing other people
- Learning to be gentle
- Integrating a new player in a game
- Making aggression-free body contact
- Having blind trust
- Showing affection

How to Play: This game is very suitable for introducing and integrating a new student, but it can also be played even if there isn't a new student. After the newcomer has been introduced, she may play the leader in a few simple games, starting with this one. All players close their eyes. The leader goes from one player to the next, "waking them up." She can do this by touching them, or with words.

Variations

- Waking up on the "snowball" principle: Every player who has been wakened goes to another player and wakes him up in the same way. Then she sits down. Only the new student (the group leader) is allowed to wake up several players.
- If the new student doesn't know the player's names she can wake them up by calling out, for example, "Girl in the blue dress and the long black hair, wake up!"

Notes

- The advantage of this game is that it gives the new student a chance to look at her classmates without herself being examined, as the other players have their eyes closed. She makes contact in whatever manner is agreeable to her, choosing between verbal and physical contact. Everybody likes to be awakened by the new student.
- It's important not to ask too much of the new student. The games suggested as follow-up games all are games that can easily be played by

beginners. Refrain from insisting that the new student answer any of the reflection questions, as she might not have any experience with these methods.

Reflections
- How do you usually wake up?
- Who wakes you in a nice way?

Follow-up Games
1–5: What I Like ◆ 45–51: Cooperation Games ◆ 53: The Grouping Game ◆ 8: Observing the Room ◆ 20: Traveling Names ◆ 26: The Seat on My Right Is Empty (with a Twist) ◆ 27–32: Perceiving You ◆ 33–40: Working with You ◆ 97–101: Pantomime Play

Follow-up Games from *101 More Life Skills Games for Children*
22–34: Getting to Know You ◆ 40–45: Working with You ◆ 60–66: Integration Games

53

The Grouping Game

Goals
- Reducing fear of meeting new people
- Noticing similarities
- Getting to know the group
- Improving visual perception
- Building trust
- Making contact

How to Play: This game is very suitable for introducing and integrating a new student, but it can also be played even if there isn't a new student. Everyone's eyes are closed, except for the newcomer's. The new student gently steers the other players into groups in different corners of the room without saying why—maybe one group all has the same color hair, maybe another is wearing shoes that don't lace. Once every player has been assigned to a group, they open their eyes and try to figure out what they have in common with the other people in their group.

Examples
- Wearing blue jeans
- Same length of hair
- Similar heights
- All have the same hair color

Variations
- An experienced player or the group leader can help the new student to divide the other players into groups.
- All players sit in a circle with their eyes closed, holding cards in front of them with their names on them. Instead of steering the players into different corners, the newcomer collects the cards and puts them in different corners of the room. The players open their eyes, find their cards and guess with the other group members what they have in common.

- In another version, the new student is treated like any other player. One player—not the new student—leaves the room. The group leader divides the remaining players into several groups. The outside player is called in and tries to guess what the members of each group have in common. In this way, if the game is played several times, the new student will naturally be integrated into several different groups. At the end, all the players say what they had in common when they were in the group with the new student.

Note: This game may potentially emphasize physical differences. If doing so is not appropriate for the group or setting, the leader should steer the class to name nonphysical characteristics.

Follow-up Games
8–19: What I Observe ◆ 27–32: Understanding You ◆ 52: Wake Up! and all of its suggested follow-up games ◆ 54: Hot Seat ◆ 87: Statue Pairs ◆ 93: Bad News and Good News Pairs

Follow-up Games from *101 More Life Skills Games for Children*
54: We Are Alike ◆ 85: Frozen Pairs

Hot Seat

Props: Paper and pens/pencils for writing

Goals
- Getting to know someone
- Initiating a conversation
- Finding commonalities
- Recognizing shared characteristics
- Recognizing differences
- Accepting secrets
- Building trust in the group

How to Play: This game is very suitable for introducing visitors to a group. For this game, cards with questions written on them need to be created—one card for each player. Depending on the age of the children, the cards can be created by either the children or the group leader. Every player draws one card from the pile and asks the newcomer the question on the card.

Examples
- How old are you?
- What are you afraid of?
- What makes you laugh?
- What is your favorite color?

Variation: The new student draws cards from the pile and asks the other players.

Role Plays: (The new student should not play the lead with these variations, unless it is her expressed wish)

- An interrogation
- Embarrassing questions from parents
- Interview with a famous person

Follow-up Games

All follow-up games suggested for 52: Wake Up! ◆ 53: The Grouping Game ◆ 55: I'm Here! ◆ 80: Praise

Follow-up Games from *101 More Life Skills Games for Children*

83: Agent Game ◆ 85–90: Statue and Sculpting Games ◆ 96: Interview

I'm Here!

Goals

- Dealing with being at the center of attention
- Tolerating body contact and closeness
- Improving acoustic perception
- Abstaining from aggression and being respectful
- Trusting others
- Integrating into the group

How to Play: This game is suitable for integrating a new person into the group. All players except the newcomer walk around the room with their eyes closed. The newcomer also walks around, but with open eyes. The group leader taps someone's shoulder. This player calls the name of the newcomer and asks, "Where are you?" The newcomer says, "I'm here!" and stops walking. All players try to find and tap the newcomer on the shoulder without opening their eyes. They can call for him once more if they still haven't found him. Once they have found him they should open their eyes

and move to the side of the room so there is more space for the remaining players.

Note: The blind players have to deal with the fact that there is less and less room the closer they get to the newcomer. Being considerate and playing together without aggression are important goals here. The newcomer has time to observe the others without being stared at.

Reflections
- You're the newcomer here. Did you feel scared when other players approached you?
- How can the group help to reduce tensions you might feel?
- What did you notice?

Follow-up Games
14: Seeing with Your Ears ◆ 20: Traveling Names ◆ 32: When It Rains, It Pours ◆ 41–44: Warming-up Games for the Group ◆ 45–51: Cooperation Games ◆ All follow-up games suggested for 52: Wake Up! ◆ 54: Hot Seat ◆ 56: Information Please ◆ 61: Cry for Help ◆ 67: Crocodile Tears ◆ 71: Animals in the Jungle ◆ 75: Polite Wild Animals

Follow-up Games from *101 More Life Skills Games for Children*
46: Punctuation Mark ◆ 52: Come into the Circle ◆ 60: Seeing with Your Fingertips ◆ 67: Groupnet ◆ 74: Something Nice ◆ 78: Jostle

Information Please

Props: Cards or other items with single letters of the alphabet written on them

Goals
- Developing sensitivity
- Developing a feeling for the group situation
- Developing group awareness
- Avoiding false modesty and boasting

How to Play: Every player chooses a letter of the alphabet (from the letter cards or wooden letters). Once everyone has a letter, they have a minute to choose a word that starts with that letter—a word that relates to the group. One by one, the players talk about the word they chose.

Examples
- **B** is for books, because we have many great books in the class.
- **C** is for clown, because sometimes Sebastian is our class clown.
- **D** is for disorder, because sometimes there is a lot of disorder in our games.
- **G** is for garbage, because sometimes there are problems in class when people leave garbage on the floor.

Variation: After playing the game, all of the players put their letters in the middle of the circle. The newcomer then grabs a few letters she remembers the descriptions for and retells them to the group.

Note: Do not embarrass the newcomer by asking her to comment on her view of the group. Her comments should be spontaneous and unsolicited. Introducing the group offers an opportunity to rethink group composition, rules, and conflicts. Visitors are a very useful means of raising group awareness.

Reflections

- As a newcomer, did you learn anything about the group?
- What impressed you the most?
- Did you notice any problems? Were they similar to problems you've noticed in other groups or classes?

Follow-up Games

54: Hot Seat and all of its suggested follow-up games

any
size

Helping Games

Solution Memory

Props: "Problem" and "solution" cards that need to be prepared in advance (see the Master Sheet that follows the game)

Goals
- Offering and accepting help
- Initiating contact and communication
- Working in pairs
- Improving social awareness
- Developing trust and dependence
- Integrating the group

How to Play: There are ten problem cards and twenty matched solution cards listed on the Master Sheet. The game is played like a game of Memory, in which players take turns turning over cards and remembering their locations in an effort to find matching pairs, but in this game players are pairing up solution and problem cards.

Variations
- Half of the players get problem cards; the other half gets solution cards. All players walk around the room. At the group leader's signal the players with problem cards ask the players with solution cards for their cards. Who finds help as fast as possible? Who offers the right solution as fast as possible?
- In small groups, the players invent their own solution memory with different cards.

Note: Even if not all cards offer very effective or original help, they initiate discussion about solving problems during the game.

Reflections
- How can you recognize an emergency situation?
- What emergency situations have you been in? What help did you get?

Follow-up Games

33–40: Working with You ◆ 41–44: Warming-up Games for the Group ◆ 45–51: Cooperation Games ◆ 58: The Comforter Game ◆ 71: Animals in the Jungle ◆ 93–96: Fairytale Games

Follow-up Games from *101 More Life Skills Games for Children*

1–10: What I'm Feeling ◆ 11–12: What I'm Thinking ◆ 22–34: Getting to Know You ◆ 40–45: Working with You ◆ 48: Lost in the Dark Woods ◆ 52–59: Cooperation Games ◆ 60–66: Integration Games ◆ 67–73: Relationship Games ◆ 74: Something Nice

Master Sheet for Solution Memory Cards

Below are the lines for the cards. The gray cards with a sad face on them are the problem cards, the white ones with a smily face on them are the solution cards.

☹ I don't have enough friends in class.	☺ Invite your classmates to a party!	☺ Try to talk about the problem with a classmate.
☹ I just don't know what's what in math.	☺ See if one of your classmates wants to come home with you. You could study and play!	☺ Ask someone else, maybe a parent, to explain concepts you are having difficulty with to see if that helps you understand things better.
☹ My parents never play anything with me.	☺ Ask them to teach you their favorite game.	☺ Put on your list of wishes for your birthday a "Play with Me" gift certificate.
☹ My father constantly turns off the TV and says, "You watch too much TV."	☺ Prove to your father that you don't watch too much by marking your shows in the TV program guide.	☺ Call your father's attention to a show both of you would like to watch.

☹ I'd like to have a nice bicycle like the other kids have.	☺ Think about how you could earn additional money doing house chores, yardwork, or by holding a garage sale.	☺ If you have a friend who owns a bike, ask if you could borrow it for a little while. You might even have a toy they would like to borrow in exchange.
☹ I don't have enough allowance.	☺ Tell your problem to a few adult relatives who you trust.	☺ Ask your parents how you could solve this problem.
☹ I failed a test.	☺ Ask the teacher if you would be able to take a makeup test and then study hard for it.	☺ Put extra effort into your homework and school exercises.
☹ My friend hasn't talked to me for three days.	☺ Make her a nice card.	☺ Say you are sad and that you'd like to talk things out.
☹ I've lost my homework.	☺ Try to redo it.	☺ Do extra homework and decorate it nicely.
☹ My father told me I'm grounded for three days.	☺ Offer your father help with some chores.	☺ Get a bunch of books and curl up with them at home.
☹ I can't find the computer game my mom gave me. I'm sure she'll never give me anything expensive again.	☺ Save money from your allowance to buy a new one.	☺ Help your mother look for something she has misplaced. She'll be pleased and will understand your situation.
☹ I did something that could get my brother and me in trouble. What if he tells our parents so they won't blame him?	☺ Try to resolve the situation, make up for it, or apologize.	☺ Confess everything to your parents yourself.

The Comforter Game

Props: "Problem slips" that need to be prepared in advance (see the Master Sheet that follows the game)

Goals
- Developing empathy
- Learning to hold a conversation
- Learning to listen
- Offering and accepting help
- Initiating contact and communication
- Integrating into the group
- Showing affection
- Developing partnership and trust
- Learning to be flexible

How to Play: Every other player gets a "problem slip" with a make-believe problem on it (see the master pages that follow this exercise) and reads it. The players who don't get problem slips are "comforters."

Each comforter talks to a person with a problem slip and asks her about her troubles, as in "Why do you look so sad today?" The problem owners talk about their make-believe misfortunes. The comforter plays the role of a friend, neighbor, teacher, mother, or any other role in which she thinks she can offer advice or help to the problem owner.

After this conversation the comforter looks for another problem owner, and so on until she has dealt with about four problems. All of these conversations are happening at the same time, and the leader doesn't try to control the various partner changes. As soon as a comforter is finished with one conversation, she looks for a new problem owner who doesn't have a partner at the moment.

A feedback round follows. In the circle, everyone reads his own problem and tells the groups about the best help they were offered, explaining why it helped them. Maybe it helped because it was an original solution to a problem, or maybe just because the helper had a really good and helpful attitude.

Follow-up Games

57: Solution Memory and all of its suggested follow-up games ◆
59: The Helper Game

Master Sheet for Comforter Game Cards

PROBLEM SLIP 1 Everyone else gets to pick how to wear their hair, but I'm wearing braids because my father wants me to. The other kids pull them and make fun of me.	PROBLEM SLIP 2 I have asthma and I'm not allowed to play sports. This makes it hard for me to make friends.	PROBLEM SLIP 3 I spend all my time on homework, so I don't play any sports. Because of that, everybody picks on me.	PROBLEM SLIP 4 I have a good report card, but I have a C in English because I don't read well. Now I have to practice reading with my parents every day, and my friends make fun of me because I need this extra help.
PROBLEM SLIP 5 I constantly get extra assignments because I lose my homework. Now people think I'm lazy.	PROBLEM SLIP 6 I'm the only one who got a D on the last spelling test. I'm sure everybody thinks I'm stupid.	PROBLEM SLIP 7 Everybody makes fun of me because I see a speech therapist for my stuttering.	PROBLEM SLIP 8 Everybody calls me "fatso" because I'm overweight. I wish I could run away.
PROBLEM SLIP 9 If somebody in class gets in trouble, they always blame me. The teacher's always on their side.	PROBLEM SLIP 10 My parents like my younger siblings better than me.	PROBLEM SLIP 11 I once stole someone's pen. It was just one time, but now everybody says I steal things.	PROBLEM SLIP 12 Next weekend I'm going on a sleepover. Everybody's going to find out that I'm a bedwetter.
PROBLEM SLIP 13 I'm the only kid in school who doesn't have a TV at home. When the others talk about what they saw on TV, I can't join in.	PROBLEM SLIP 14 I've only been in this school for two weeks because we just moved. I still don't have any friends here.	PROBLEM SLIP 15 I have to wear hand-me-downs from my brothers, so everyone makes fun of me for wearing clothes that are not in style.	PROBLEM SLIP 16 Everybody makes fun of me because both my parents work and can't pick me up from school.

Helping Games

The Helper Game

Props: Images of children in emergency situations for all players; helper cards that need to be prepared in advance

Goals
- Raising problem awareness
- Offering and accepting help
- Initiating contact and communication
- Enhancing creativity
- Deepening the group relationship
- Developing social awareness and empathy

How to Play: Every player receives a picture of a child in an emergency situation, such as alone on a city street at night or hanging from a window or cliff. These can be photographs, pictures cut from magazines, or drawings. Or they could even be photographs taken in a sculpting game (see

Games #84–92 or the section of Statue and Sculpting Games in *101 More Life Skills Games for Children* (Games #85–90).

In addition to the emergency pictures, there are four times as many helper cards with objects drawn on them such as a house, a bunch of flowers, a string, a helicopter, a medicine bottle, a hammer.

One player starts by describing her emergency situation, starting with "I…." The other players in turn give her a picture with an object and give reasons why the object might be helpful.

Examples
- I am afraid to be home alone in bed.
- I am face to face with a bully on a deserted street.
- I just broke the neighbor's window.

Reflections
- Did you prefer to accept help from group members who are your friends?
- How did you deal with offers that weren't really helpful?

Variations
- The pictures and helper cards are shuffled. Every player chooses a picture and a helper card. Since there are fewer helper card options, players sometimes have to be very creative in order to help someone, or they have to pass.
- Instead of pictures, in a group of older players the emergency situation can be described in several sentences on a slip of paper. These slips are passed out.

Follow-up Games
57: Solution Memory and all of its suggested follow-up games ◆
58: The Comforter Game ◆ 60: Friendly Exam

Friendly Exam

Props: A blackboard, chalk, and a teacher's desk

Goals
- Reducing exam fears
- Accepting and offering help
- Dealing with competition
- Fostering unity and group spirit
- Making eye contact

How to Play: Taking an exam is such a lonely thing. Wouldn't it be great if instead of having to come up with all the answers by ourselves, we could get help from our friends? One problem: we wouldn't learn anything! Oh well—we can dream, can't we? So here's what an exam in a dream might be like.

One player has to take the exam. He leaves the room. The teacher writes difficult questions on the board, then sits down facing the board. The other players are sitting behind his back. The student who has to take the exam comes back and stands between the teacher and the board. The teacher reads him the exam questions. As he tries to answer, the other players help with all kinds of clues—hand motions, whispering.

Example: How long ago did the dinosaurs roam the earth?

Reflections
- Are you afraid when you take an exam?
- Was anyone afraid just now?
- What is the difference between a role-play like this and a real exam?
- What makes exams so scary?
- Which situations in everyday life are like exams?
- If you studied hard for an exam and knew all of the material, would it be fun?

Role Plays

- I didn't pass the exam. What now?
- Entrance examination for a strange club

Follow-up Games

6–7: What I Can Do ◆ 33–40: Working with You ◆ 45–51: Cooperation Games ◆ 59: The Helper Game ◆ 61: Cry for Help ◆ 72: Tug
of War II ◆ 73: I-You-We Dice ◆ 75: Polite Wild Animals ◆ 74: Slo-
Mo Tennis ◆ 79: Rumors ◆ 82: Vampire ◆ 97–101: Pantomime
Play

Follow-up Games from *101 More Life Skills Games for Children*

11–12: What I'm Thinking ◆ 30: Heads Are Truthful, Tails Lie ◆
40–45: Working with You ◆ 75: President of Praise ◆ 77: Circle of
Threat

Cry for Help

Goals

- Giving and accepting help
- Making aggression-free body contact
- Developing trust
- Showing affection
- Warming up
- Making contact and improving communication
- Developing group spirit
- Improving social awareness

How to Play: Form three groups, numbered 1, 2, and 3. All players randomly walk about in the room. The group leader calls a group name, for example "Group 3!" All members of group 3 shout, moan, or cry for help, then pretend to sit down, fall over, and pass out in slow motion. The members of

groups 1 and 2 run to catch these players and keep them from falling. Whoever falls is revived by several players and carefully helped back up. After a while the group leader calls the number of another group and the game continues.

Reflections
- What other kinds of crying for help are there?
- What's an example of a cry for help that wasn't heard?

Role Play: A family is sitting at home in the evening. It's quiet. All of a sudden, they think they've heard a cry for help out in the streets. They speculate what it could be. What should be done?

Follow-up Games
47: Boom Box ◆ 57: Solution Memory and all of its suggested follow-up games ◆ 60: Friendly Exam ◆ 62: The Emergency Kit ◆ 75: Polite Wild Animals ◆ 77: Frontline ◆ 81: Ghosts and Travelers ◆ 82: Vampire ◆ 83: Wolf in Sheep's Clothing

Follow-up Games from *101 More Life Skills Games for Children*
77: Circle of Threat ◆ 80: Face-off

Emergency Kit

Props: Paper and pens/pencils for writing/drawing; magazines and scissors (optional); suitcase or travel bag

Goals
- Offering help
- Improving social awareness
- Expressing unity and affection
- Developing thoughtfulness in giving
- Improving relationships and developing group spirit

How to Play: This game is meant to be used when a child is about to go on a journey or move away from the area.

Each of the other players writes down something on a slip of paper that might help her on the trip. It can also be a picture, a photo, or a drawing. One after another, players put their slips into a suitcase or travel bag at the center of the circle and explain how their suggestion might help the traveler.

Variation: Instead of going on a journey by herself, the student is moving with her parents to another state.

Reflections
- Which gifts were you most pleased with?
- How well do your classmates know you?

Follow-up Games
1–5: What I Like ◆ 45–51: Cooperation Games ◆ 61: Cry for Help ◆ 63: I Fell in the Well

Follow-up Games from *101 More Life Skills Games for Children*
26: Hello, Goodbye ◆ 34: Picture Present ◆ 35: Yes No Yes No ◆ 67–73: Relationship Games

any size

Helping Games

63

I Fell
in the Well

Goals
- Helping others
- Showing affection
- Enhancing creativity and agility
- Developing partnerships

How to Play: One player stands in the center of the circle. Suddenly, she sits down on the floor and cries, "I fell in the well!" The other players ask: "Who should pull you out?" The fallen player answers by describing a contest in which, for example, the person who makes the funniest face or laughs the loudest or holds their breath the longest, wins. The fallen player picks her "helper" based on who performed the designated task best. The

helper now pulls the fallen player out of the well, and then it's the helper's turn to fall in.

Follow-up Games
All follow-up games suggested for 57: Solution Memory ◆ 62: The Emergency Kit ◆ 64: Bodyguards

Bodyguards

Goals
- Developing strength and unity
- Winning and losing without aggression
- Learning to cooperate
- Dealing with integration and disability in a group
- Being dependent on the group
- Developing trust in the group
- Seeking sanctuary when afraid

How to Play: Someone is chosen to be "It" and goes to the middle of the room. The other players stand on one side of the room. One of them volunteers to be the "celebrity." "It" is told who the celebrity is. The game is that the group tries to walk to the other side of the room, while "It," who is also walking, tries to tag the celebrity and the group tries to prevent this. If "It" accidentally touches anyone in the group while "It" is reaching for the celebrity, they have to freeze or sit down for five seconds. Nobody should be hurt or pushed aggressively during the game.

Variation: "It" doesn't know who celebrity is. He touches as many players as possible—he might just tag the right one.

Note: This game is perhaps better suited to a larger, more open space than a classroom.

Reflections
- How does it feel to be the celebrity?
- Do bodyguards sometimes need protection too?
- Have you ever felt weak?
- What helped you?
- How were you helped?
- Were you able to help yourself?

Follow-up Games
63: I Fell in the Well ◆ 65: Brother, Help! Sister, Help! ◆ 75: Polite

Wild Animals ◆ 79: Rumors ◆ 80: Praise ◆ 81: Ghosts and
Travelers ◆ 82: Vampire ◆ 83: Wolf in Sheep's Clothing ◆
93–96: Fairytale Games

Follow-up Games from *101 More Life Skills Games for Children*
48: Lost in the Dark Woods ◆ 49: Stumbling over Roots ◆
50: Through the Thicket ◆ 52–59: Cooperation Games ◆
60–66: Integration Games ◆ 74–84: Aggression Games

Brother, Help!
Sister, Help!

Goals

- Seeking and giving help
- Showing affection and dependence
- Developing unity and partnership
- Fostering cooperation and group spirit
- Integrating the group

How to Play: A game of tag, with an important twist. One player is chosen to be "It," and tries to tag the other players. A player who is about to be tagged can reach out for another player's hand and shout "Brother, help!" or "Sister, help!" A player holding another player's hand when he is tagged is "safe." If a player is caught and isn't holding hands with anyone, she

becomes "It." In order to keep the game moving, players can hold hands for a maximum of 10 seconds.

Reflections

- When was the last time you asked someone for help?
- Can you always ask someone for help, like you can in this game?
- In this game, the help-seeker cannot be ignored. Is it easier to ignore someone who needs help in real life?
- Is it always that easy to help?
- There is an expression, "reaching out for help." What does it mean?

Follow-up Games

5: Good Fairy ◆ 31: You Move Me ◆ 33–40: Working with You ◆
45–51: Cooperation Games ◆ 66: Freeze Tag ◆ 64: Bodyguards ◆
77: Frontline ◆ 93–96: Fairytale Games

Follow-up Games from *101 More Life Skills Games for Children*

20: Pieces of Personality ◆ 40–45: Working with You ◆
60–66: Integration Games ◆ 74–84: Aggression Games

Freeze Tag

Goals
- Being helpful
- Showing affection
- Fostering solidarity and partnership
- Fostering cooperation
- Integrating the group

How to Play: One player is "It". Any person he touches "freezes"—that is, stops moving in whatever position he was in when he was touched. Other players can bring him back to life by touching him and shouting "Free!" The freed player can now continue running.

Variations
- Whoever is frozen stands with his feet apart. He gets freed when another player crawls through his legs.
- Frozen players can be freed if they are carried piggyback to the "hospital" (a corner of the room). They cannot be caught while being carried.
- Frozen players can be released if two players holding hands surround them.

Reflections
- Are there players who feel they weren't helped enough?
- What does it feel like to wait for help?
- What does it feel like to free someone?
- Are there situations in real life in which one is waiting to be let free?
- Name situations in life in which it is easy to free someone.

Follow-up Games
All follow-up games suggested for 57: Solution Memory ◆ 65: Brother, Help! Sister, Help! ◆ 67: Crocodile Tears

Helping Games

Crocodile Tears

Props: A balloon

Goals
- Making aggression-free body contact
- Giving and accepting help
- Fostering partnership and solidarity
- Patiently trusting in help
- Showing affection by helping

How to Play: Before starting, ask for children to volunteer to "get hurt" during the game and choose a player to be "It." The players walk around the room. Whoever is "It" tags people by touching them on the arms, legs, or head with a balloon. The player who gets tagged pretends to cry until another player puts a pretend bandage on the spot touched by the balloon. The injured person is crying too hard to show or tell the helper where she was injured—but she stops crying as soon as the helper guesses the injured spot. Players can start walking around again after they get their pretend bandage. Helpers may not be tagged while they are helping someone.

Variation: Ask for a player to volunteer to be a "victim." After the victim is chosen, one player whispers a pretend insult into her ear. In response, the victim starts sobbing. The other players help by asking questions to find out what had happened or what was said. The insulted player may only respond with "Yes" or "No." Once they know why the player is upset, the players then help the injured person by comforting him.

Reflections
- When was the last time somebody hurt you on purpose?
- Is anyone entitled to inflict physical pain on others? Tell us about incidents in which you unintentionally inflicted physical pain on someone. There is also emotional pain. Give examples!
- Could emotional pain be worse than physical pain?

- Can emotional pain be prevented?
- How can you protect yourself from emotional pain?
- How can emotional pain be treated?

Role Plays
- Fight in the schoolyard.
- You did that on purpose!

Follow-up Games
All follow-up games suggested for 61: Cry for Help ◆ 68: Moving Help
◆ 66: Freeze Tag

Moving Help

Goals
- Giving and accepting help
- Developing patience while helping others
- Communicating nonverbally
- Developing cooperation and group spirit
- Developing partnership
- Developing sensitivity and empathy

How to Play: In pantomime, one player shows an object that is difficult to move. He carries, drags, or pushes it. As soon as another player thinks she knows what the object is, she joins in. The other player, in pantomime, can correct her if he thinks she's thinking of a different object. He can also show her where and how to hold it. The object can even be put down temporarily. The helper can be sent away if she acts clumsily. Several players can help at the same time. Their goal is to reach the other side of the room. When they do, every helper writes the name of the object on a slip of paper and compares slips. Then, the players who were watching try to guess what the object was.

Variation: Help someone build a house in pantomime.

Note: In pantomime games, large, slow movements are best. Previous experience with pantomime can be advantageous (e.g., Getting Stronger, Game #97).

Reflections
- Did everyone guess it was the same object, or did one person think they were dragging an elephant while someone else thought it was a water glass?
- Did you realize that your help was needed? Did you assist each other well?
- How did you communicate?

- Was it easy to guide the helper?
- Did the helper help too much? Did you need a lot of patience for each other?

Role Plays
- How come I always have to help?
- Let me do it myself!
- If you don't want to help, I don't need your help!

Follow-up Games
33–40: Working with You ◆ 67: Crocodile Tears ◆ 69: Carrying Contest ◆ 84–92: Statue and Sculpting Games ◆ 97–101: Pantomime Play

Follow-up Games from *101 More Life Skills Games for Children*
40–45: Working with You ◆ 85–90: Statue and Sculpting Games

Carrying Contest

Goals

- Developing partnership and skillful cooperation
- Coordinating activities
- Dealing with the pressures of performance and competition
- Dealing with winning and losing
- Planning
- Depending on a partner

How to Play: This is a game for the gym. The group leader divides the players into pairs. She instructs them to carry two long duffel bags (they can be filled with pillows or sandbags, depending on the age of the group) from one end of the gym to the other. The second duffle bag must not be moved before the first one has touched the opposite wall. Every pair gets only one turn.

The leader points out to the group that there are different ways to accomplish this mission: The two bags can be carried separately by different partners, or they can be carried jointly one after the other. Each pair has a meeting and then tells the referee which variation they have chosen.

The players can establish records using a stopwatch. Who was the fastest to transport a duffel bag by herself? Which pair transported it the fastest? Which pair carried two in a row the fastest? Which pair was the fastest in carrying the duffel bags individually one after another (if both times are added together)?

The referee enters the achieved times in a chart, and after every pair has gone, the group leader holds an informal awards ceremony. The leader then arranges the players into different pairs so players have an opportunity to set a record with a different partner.

Notes

- Playing the game a second time is important because it allows the players to apply what they learned in the first round. Learning leads to changes in behavior.

- This game can also be played in a park with a start and a finish line.

Reflections
- How did you choose a method the first time? Did one of you decide, or did you decide together?
- Did you help each other?
- Do you know your partner better now?
- How did having a partner affect you?

Follow-up Games
All follow-up games suggested for 57: Solution Memory ◆ 68: Moving Help ◆ 70: First Day of School

First Day of School

Props: Objects or pictures that can be loosely associated with something related to the school year; a bag or backpack

Goals
- Coping with fears about school
- Expressing wishes
- Enhancing creativity
- Developing optimism
- Developing group spirit

How to Play: The group leader puts a lot of objects or pictures and an empty bag or backpack in the center of the circle. Every object or picture symbolizes (directly or indirectly) a wish for the new school year. Each student in turn takes one object and puts it into the group's backpack, explaining what wish the object symbolizes.

Examples
- Alarm clock (being on time)
- Pencil (writing stories)
- Sunblock (good weather)
- Piece of wood (patient teacher)

Variations
- Wishes can be written on slips of paper. The slips of paper can be kept and referred to at the end of the year. Did any of the wishes come true?
- This game can also be played as a "Gift Game." Players give each other "wishes" and "gifts" for the school year.
- The students' wishes for the school year can be compared to wishes the teacher has prepared.

Follow-up Games

1–5: What I Like ◆ 41–44: Warming-up Games for the Group ◆ 45–51: Cooperation Games ◆ 69: Carrying Contest

Follow-up Games from *101 More Life Skills Games for Children*

1–10: What I'm Feeling ◆ 22–34: Getting to Know You ◆ 40–45: Working with You ◆ 46–51: Warming-up Games for the Group ◆ 56: Designing a Classroom ◆ 67–73: Relationship Games ◆ 74–84: Aggression Games

Animals in the Jungle

Goals
- Making aggression-free body contact
- Developing trust in other players
- Being comfortable with physical contact
- Developing empathy and consideration
- Enhancing communication skills

How to Play: The players sit in a circle. Everybody imitates the group leader. The group leader puts her hands on the floor and makes them into fists. Then she says: "An elephant is walking through the jungle." (Everyone's fists are banging on the floor.) "It walks up a mountain and reaches a plain." (Everybody's fists march up their legs and thighs). "It turns to the right" (Everybody's fists are lightly hitting the back of the person sitting to their right.) "It walks to the left." (All players move their fists away from their neighbor on the right, across their own thighs, and back to the person sitting to their left.) "It walks back into the jungle." (Everybody marches their fists down their own thighs and back to the floor.) "The elephant meets a rabbit." (The hands hop across the floor.) "The rabbit runs up a mountain." (And now with hands hopping instead of fists banging, the steps are repeated.)

Other animals: lions, snakes, flamingos, gorillas....

Note: The group leader points out that nobody must be rough. This can happen unintentionally with some children who have a hard time assessing how intense their touching is. It's helpful if the children try out the different animals on the floor and on their own bodies first. Also, you will find that come children will not like hard touches while others will not like soft touches.

Reflections
- Which touches did you like, and which ones did you not like?

- With which animals was it difficult not to be rough?
- Did you notice differences between your neighbors?

Follow-up Games

27–32: Perceiving You ◆ 33–40: Working with You ◆ 41–44: Warming-up Games for the Group ◆ 45–51: Cooperation Games ◆ 52: Wake Up! ◆ 61: Cry for Help ◆ 72: Tug of War II ◆ 88: Mannequins

Follow-up Games from *101 More Life Skills Games for Children*

25: Zip Zap Names ◆ 40–45: Working with You ◆ 48: Lost in the Dark Woods ◆ 49: Stumbling over Roots ◆ 50: Through the Thicket ◆ 74: Something Nice

Tug of War II

Props: Strong rope at least 10–15 feet long; cushions and/or mattresses (optional)

Goals
- Learning to cooperate
- Developing solidarity
- Integrating outsiders
- Helping other people
- Experiencing victory and defeat

How to Play: Every player gets a number. All the players are seated in a circle, with a rope on the floor in the center of the group. The group leader calls out two numbers, an odd and an even one. The players with those numbers grab the rope and start pulling in opposite directions. Other players can then spontaneously join in and help them—players with even numbers helping the even-numbered player, players with odd numbers helping the odd-numbered player.

Note: A lot of room is needed for this game (gym or outdoors). Cushions and/or mattresses may be needed for safety.

Reflections
- Why did the winning team win?
- How did the game go, from the perspective of the team leader? Is he disappointed or pleased about the help offered? Did he feel let down?
- Did the joy of teamwork offset the disappointment of losing?

Follow-up Games
6–7: What I Can Do ◆ 27–32: Understanding You ◆ 73: I-You-We Dice ◆ 71: Animals in the Jungle and all of its suggested follow-up games

I-You-We Dice

Props: A modified die (see below); action cards (optional, see the Master Sheet that follows the game)

Goals
- Dealing with aggression
- Learning empathetic behavior
- Reducing shyness
- Showing consideration, trust, tolerance, and affection
- Improving communication

How to Play: A special kind of die is prepared by placing stickers over a regular one. Instead of the numbers 1–6, now two sides of the die will say "I," two sides will say "You," and the remaining two will say "We."

Every player thinks of an activity that another player could carry out in front of the group. This activity must not be painful, embarrassing, or too difficult.

All players in the circle take turns naming the activity that they have thought up. After they say what the activity is, they throw the die. If the die shows the "I"-side, they have to do the activity themselves. If it shows the "You"-side, they designate another player to do it. If it shows the "We"-side, everybody plays.

Examples
- Shake hands with or give a high five to another player.
- Hop or stand on one leg.
- Tell the group what you want to be when you grow up.

Variation: This game can be played as a board game in small groups and is especially good for older children. The action cards (see the end of this game) are cut out. On a piece of cardboard, 18 game-board spaces are drawn in a circle. Every third space is an action space, on top of which three action cards are placed face down. One space is designated as the starting point for the game.

The game is played with a regular die and playing pieces that are moved according to the number shown when the die is thrown. If a playing piece reaches an action space, the player also rolls the I-You-We die. After the activity has been carried out, the card is put under the action field pile. The game can continue indefinitely as the 18 fields on the board are arranged in a circle. The players can also make additional cards.

Note: The I-You-We die is a way to make sure that the activities can actually be carried out because the player who devises them knows that he might have to carry it out himself.

Follow-up Games
3: Wishing Cards ◆ 20–40: You-Games ◆ 41–44: Warming up Games for the Group ◆ 52–56: Integrating New Classmates ◆ 57–70: Helping Games ◆ 72: Tug of War II ◆ 74: Slo-Mo Tennis ◆ 84–92: Statue and Sculpting Games

Follow-up Games from *101 More Life Skills Games for Children*
22–45: You-Games ◆ 52–59: Cooperation Games ◆ 67–73: Relationship Games ◆ 74–84: Aggression Games ◆ 85–90: Statue and Sculpting Games

Master Sheet for Optional Action Cards

Shake hands with another player.	Say something nice into your neighbor's ear.	Tell the person next to you something nice about someone else.
Tap another player gently on the shoulder.	Tell another player where you would like to go on vacation.	Choose a player that you'd like to sit next to.
Greet a player in a nice way, as if you haven't seen each other in a long time.	Say something nice about each player.	Do a short role-play with one of the other players: You have upset her and try everything to patch things up with her.

Give another player a high-five.	Ask a player to choose an action card for you.	Play a short role-play with one of the other players. She is sad and you try to find out why, so you can comfort her.
Tell the group what you want to be when you grow up.	Tell the person sitting on your left what you would buy him if you had a lot of money.	Choose a player with whom you would like to carry a third player around the room.
Look for an object in the room that the player sitting on your right would like to have as decoration.	Give all the players a gentle, friendly hug.	Tell another player a joke.

Slo-Mo Tennis

Goals
- Renouncing and reducing aggressive behavior
- Dealing with anger about a defeat
- Controlling movement
- Learning fair behavior as a winner
- Dealing with competition
- Accepting other people's abilities and weaknesses

How to Play: Two players pretend to play tennis in slow motion. There is an umpire who blows a whistle to indicate the start of every game. After the players play a few games, the umpire chooses the winner based on which player most clearly moved in slow motion.

Variation: Two groups move toward each other in slow motion. When they meet, they start fighting in slow motion. Before the game, the group leader has determined which group will lose. If the players want to play another round, the group that won last time plays the losing team. The winning team shows their joy over winning in slow motion and pantomime. How does the losing team behave?

Reflections
- What feelings did you have when you won? What did you feel when you saw your opponent happy about their victory when you lost?
- What effect does it have on the group if you win together?
- In which everyday games do you have big chances of winning?
- Are there fighting games that you'd rather avoid? Do fighting games make you tense?
- After contact sports, have you been angry with the opponent?
- What behavior do you like to see in a winner or loser?
- Do you like watching martial arts?

Note: Playing in slow motion is particularly difficult. A good practice exercise can be a foot race in slow motion. At a signal from the game leader, five players start simultaneously from one side of the room. The movements should resemble those of a 100-yard dash, and it is a requirement that the movement never come to a halt. Whoever stops moving is out of the game. The last player to reach the other side of the room wins.

Role Plays

- It's unfair that I lost!
- It's your fault that we lost!
- He started it!
- An unequal fight.

Follow-up Games

31: You Move Me ♦ 32: When It Rains, It Pours ♦ 33–40: Working with You ♦ 43: Greeting Game ♦ 44: Good Morning! ♦ 50: Tug of War ♦ 64: Bodyguards ♦ 67: Crocodile Tears ♦ 73: I-You-We Dice ♦ 75: Polite Wild Animals ♦ 77: Frontline ♦ 81: Ghosts and Travelers ♦ 82: Vampire

Follow-up Games from *101 More Life Skills Games for Children*

40–45: Working with You ♦ 48: Lost in the Dark Woods ♦ 79: War Dance ♦ 80: Face-off

Polite Wild Animals

Goals
- Reducing aggressive behavior
- Dealing with fear
- Recognizing the group as protective

How to Play: All players move around on the floor like wild animals. When they encounter each other they behave aggressively—but without touching each other.

Variations
- A group of cats and a group of dogs meet.
- The group is divided into three small groups: Groups A and B form fantastic monsters with many legs and arms together. Group C moves around and reacts to these roaring and menacing monsters.
- The group is divided into four small groups. Each group forms a single monster. They meet and mock-fight with each other
- Two monsters meet. They roar back and forth at each other.
- A volunteer is sitting in a Stone Age cave in the middle of the room. Six players form the cave. At the group leader's signal, an animal approaches the cave. It can sneak around the cave, it can creep into the

cave through a hole, and it can touch the cave dweller, but it must not hurt her. At the group leader's signal, the animal retreats to the side of the room, and a new animal takes a turn approaching the cave dweller.

Notes
- The players must not yell into each other's ears. If the game becomes too aggressive, the group leader can use the commands "slow motion" or "freeze!"
- After this game, a fun movement game (see games 41–44, the Warming-up Games) should be played for relaxation. If the players need to focus on work afterwards, a concentration game can be played in the end.

Reflections
- What was scariest for you: roaring or quiet snarling? Sudden silence? The closeness of an animal? The frightening sight of it? Was it a sneaky approach or a ferocious one?
- What did you do to relieve the tension?
- What behaviors of other people in everyday life do you find threatening?
- Are you afraid of certain animals in everyday life?
- Were you able to make an impact as a wild animal?
- Do you enjoy impressing other people?

Role Play: "Stone Age people": a scout rushes into the cave and reports an approaching pack of wild animals. The group quickly decides on protective measures.

Follow-up Games
74: Slo-Mo Tennis ◆ 76: Detective ◆ 77: Frontline ◆ 78: Peace Language ◆ 81: Ghosts and Travelers ◆ 82: Vampire ◆ 83: Wolf in Sheep's Clothing ◆ 45–51: Cooperation Games ◆ 84–92: Statue and Sculpting Games

Follow-up Games from *101 More Life Skills Games for Children*
46–51:Warming-up Games for the Group ◆ 77: Circle of Threat ◆ 78: Jostle ◆ 79: War Dance ◆ 80: Face-off ◆ 81: Gauntlet

Detective

Props: Paper and pens/pencils for writing; tape; cards from the game Memory or any other set of cards in which each card has one match

Goals
- Dealing with mistrust and suspicion
- Dealing with feelings of guilt and bad conscience
- Dealing with fear of discovery

How to Play: There are two groups of players: The criminals are in Group A and the detectives are in Group B. The group leader gives the players of Group A Memory cards that they hold in their hands, visible to all. The players of Group B get Memory cards that match the ones in Group A. However, the players in Group B do not show their cards. Each detective in Group B knows now which player in Group A they have to trail without raising any suspicion. The detectives have to find out which crime the players in Group A have committed. For that purpose, each criminal imagines a crime including the time and place they committed it, write it down on a strip of paper, and then cut the paper up into individual words. Then they tape the words onto different parts of their clothes. Now all players walk around in the room. As inconspicuously as possible, the detectives try to read the words pinned onto their criminals. As soon as they have managed to read them, they arrest the criminals, telling them the crime they committed. The criminals can make the detectives drop out of the game by telling them they know they're being shadowed by them.

Example:

On June 18th I robbed a jewelry shop on Market Street.

Reflections
- Have you ever been afraid of being found out long after getting into mischief?
- How do you deal with peoples' mistrust of you?

- How do you deal with mistakes you make?
- Do you find it difficult to admit it when you've done something wrong?
- Who can you tell about your mistake?
- What mistake or wrongdoing would you never dare to admit to having done?

Role Plays

- You admit a bad mistake to a friend. She tries to convince you to clear things up by confessing everything to your parents.
- A wallet was stolen in the class. Everybody suspects everyone else. You feel some of your classmates are secretly suspecting you.
- You have a strong suspicion that a certain classmate participated in scrawling graffiti on the school building wall.

Follow-up Games

60: Friendly Exam ◆ 65: Brother, Help! Sister, Help! ◆ 66: Freeze Tag ◆ 75: Polite Wild Animals ◆ 79: Rumors

Follow-up Games from *101 More Life Skills Games for Children*

30: Heads Are Truthful, Tails Lie ◆ 31: Rumor Factory ◆ 35: Yes No Yes No ◆ 36: Spy ◆ 38: 20 Questions ◆ 39: Two Peas in a Pod ◆ 82: Security Guard ◆ 83: Agent Game ◆ 84: Chase

Frontline

Goals
- Reducing and renouncing aggressive behavior
- Being protected by the group
- Coordinating movement and cooperation in the group
- Experimenting with closeness and distance

How to Play: Every player chooses a partner. Each partner goes to opposite sides of the room and then faces their partner so they form two rows or "frontlines" facing each other. Each line has a few minutes to decide on a rhythmical "combat" step. This can be accompanied by rhythmical clapping of the hands and other sounds. When they are ready, the two frontlines start

moving toward each other. Frontline A does a few steps and then stops. Frontline B responds by moving a few steps forward and then stops. Frontline A marches forward again. When both groups are very close to each other, face-to-face, they start moving backward, taking turns in their rhythmical backing off.

Variations

- A small group is confronted by a large one.
- A group of drummers supports the line of fighters.
- Individual observers stand in the middle of the room. How dangerous is the situation for them?
- The two groups approach each other to the accompaniment of aggressive/neutral/soft music. This variation can also be played for relaxation at the end of the game.

Note: In order to avoid true opposition, only partners who like each other should be positioned against each other. Even so, a somewhat aggressive atmosphere tends to develop that gives us an opportunity, in a safe way, to reflect on the conditions that foster aggression.

Reflections

- Did you feel good or was the game unpleasant for you?
- Do you know what music makes you feel aggressive?
- Have you seen TV shows with similar situations? What effect does it have on you to watch them?
- What influence did the behavior of players next to you have?

Role Play: Radio journalists report live from a demonstration that is taking place in a city.

Follow-up Games
74: Slo-Mo Tennis ◆ 75: Polite Wild Animals ◆ 76: Detective ◆ 45–51: Cooperation Games ◆ 78: Peace Language ◆ 91: Acting Out Pictures

Follow-up Games from *101 More Life Skills Games for Children*
79: War Dance ◆ 80: Face-off ◆ 81: Gauntlet

Peace Language

Props: "Peace Cards," which need to be prepared in advance (see Master Sheet)

Goals
- Expressing peaceful behavior verbally and nonverbally
- Observing and understanding body language
- Expressing feelings and intentions through body language
- Expressing affection and dislike
- Training social awareness
- Recognizing contradictions between body language and verbal expression

How to Play: The players divide into groups of four. The object of the game is for the players to think of a way to communicate peaceful intentions using sign language. Each group gets 16 Peace Cards from which they choose four. They then invent signs to communicate the message on the card. One player demonstrates these signs as clearly as possible for the other players, who then try to guess what the performer is trying to express.

Variations
- Incongruent behavior: One player draws a Peace Card, reads the sentence, but expresses something different through gestures and facial expressions.
- The players make drawings that symbolize the sentences on the Peace Cards. Then the other groups try to guess the meaning, just like with the signs.

Reflections
- How did your game partners react to your behavior?
- How can you recognize peaceful intentions?
- Can you always trust body language?

Follow-up Games

7: Guess What I Can Do ◆ 33–40: Working with You ◆
45–51: Cooperation Games ◆ 57–70: Helping Games ◆
77: Frontline ◆ 80: Praise ◆ 84–92: Statue and Sculpting Games ◆
97–101: Pantomime Play

Follow-up Games from *101 More Life Skills Games for Children*

4: Body Language Spells Your Mood ◆ 36: Spy ◆ 79: War Dance ◆
80: Face-off

Master Sheet

Each of the following 16 lines is on a separate card.

Look at me, I'm not armed.	I wouldn't hurt a fly.	Help me please!	I'm putting my fate into your hands.
It's safe for you to come closer.	Come, I'll take you to dinner.	I'd like to have you as a friend.	Please be peaceful.
I trust you.	Come into my house and be my guest.	Let's be friends again.	I respect you.
I'm in a good mood.	I like you.	Look, I'm putting down my weapons.	There is room for everyone here.

Aggression Games

Rumors

Goals
- Identifying outsiders and bad rumors
- Dealing with rejection
- Feeling closeness and distance
- Reacting to injustice
- Dealing with feelings of guilt

How to Play: The players stand in a circle. A volunteer slowly walks around inside the circle. The other players whisper pretend nasty rumors into each other's ears as she passes them. The volunteer then reflects on how she felt when everyone was telling nasty rumors about her.

Examples
- "He's a thief! He's a thief!"
- "It's his fault! It's his fault!"

Note: The first two or three volunteers should be popular children who don't easily lose their composure.

Reflections
- Have you ever felt suspected or accused of something? How can you deal with such situations? Who could support you? Who could you count on?
- Are you easily influenced by rumors?

Role Plays
- Accusation and defense: One half of the players play prosecutors, the other half tries to find arguments and evidence against every sentence of the accusers.
- Sequence of scenes: arrest by the police in the middle of the street—people murmuring—a crowd in front of the court room—accusation and defense—conviction—press conference.

Follow-up Games

20: Traveling Names ◆ 57: Solution Memory ◆ 58: The Comforter Game ◆ 59: The Helper Game ◆ 60: Friendly Exam ◆ 78: Peace Language ◆ 80: Praise

Follow-up Games from *101 More Life Skills Games for Children*

31: Rumor Factory ◆ 67–73: Relationship Games ◆ 75: President of Praise ◆ 77: Circle of Threat ◆ 78: Jostle ◆ 79: War Dance ◆ 81: Gauntlet ◆ 82: Security Guard

Praise

Goals
- Dealing with admiration
- Feeling closeness and distance
- Developing humility

How to Play: The players stand in a circle. A volunteer slowly walks around inside the circle. The other players whisper praise for that person into each other's ears as he passes them. The volunteer then reflects on how it felt when everyone was whispering nice things about them.

Examples
- "He's really smart! He's really smart!"
- "He's cute! He's cute!"

Reflection: How did you feel when everyone was praising you?

Role Plays
- Appearance of a great star: Interview
- Press conference of a politician/star

Follow-up Games
All follow-up games suggested for 79: Rumors

Ghosts and Travelers

Goals
- Dealing with fear of aggression
- Reducing and renouncing aggression
- Showing fairness toward disadvantaged players
- Trusting in fairness
- Training perception

How to Play: The players are divided into two groups: a group of ghosts and a group of travelers (anxious children are encouraged to be ghosts instead of travelers). The ghosts position themselves to form a haunted tunnel or pathway through the room. The travelers pair off. One traveler leads her partner, whose eyes are closed, by the hand along this haunted pathway. The ghosts howl, sigh, and make spooky sounds aimed at the traveler who has her eyes closed. The traveler tries not to open her eyes until she gets to the end of the path.

Variation: Princess in the Haunted Tunnel: Three guides surround a princess as she walks through the haunted tunnel. They gently try to keep the worst horror away from the princess.

Reflections
- Were you anxious or amused?
- If you were frightened, why do you think that is?
- Did your guide provide security?
- Were there unfair ghosts?
- What particularly scared you?
- Did the ghosts enjoy their role?
- What frightens you in everyday life?
- Do you know people who enjoy scaring other people?

Role Plays
- When the light went out in the basement
- Unauthorized visit to the old castle
- Alone at home at night
- The night I made the ghosts afraid

Follow-up Games
82: Vampire and all of its suggested follow-up games

Aggression Games

Vampire

Goals
- Reducing fear of aggression

How to Play: All players walk around the room blindfolded. The group leader inconspicuously taps one player's shoulder. This player now knows she is the vampire, but she keeps walking and keeps her eyes closed. When she encounters another player, she puts her hands on his shoulder to indicate that the person is being turned into a vampire. The new vampire then gives a blood-curdling scream. He is now also a vampire who walks around blind, touches his victims, and makes them vampires. If two vampires meet, they touch one another and then give a deep sigh of relief. They are now no longer vampires and can become victims again.

Notes
- This game is not for people with weak nerves! After this game, it is advisable to play a game to calm down, such as a movement game with music (see "Warming-up Games").

- This game should be played in a space where it would not disturb other classes or groups.

Reflections
- Were you afraid of the first contact with a vampire?
- What effect did the sudden screams around you have on you?
- Did your own screaming give you any relief?
- What was it like to play the role of the vampire?
- Were you able to get used to the terror?
- What real-life experiences have terrified you? How can you protect yourself against that fear?
- Are there situations at school that you are afraid of?
- Are there situations in which you feel paralyzed?

Follow-up Games
83: Wolf in Sheep's Clothing ◆ 81: Ghosts and Travelers ◆ 75: Polite Wild Animals ◆ 71: Animals in the Jungle ◆ 32: When It Rains, It Pours ◆ 43: Greeting Game ◆ 52: Wake Up! ◆ 55: I'm Here! ◆ 61: Cry for Help ◆ 67: Crocodile Tears ◆ 65: Brother, Help! Sister, Help!

Follow-up Games from *101 More Life Skills Games for Children*
51: The Goofy Game ◆ 64: Blind Pool ◆ 77: Circle of Threat ◆ 83: Agent Game ◆ 84: Chase

Wolf in Sheep's Clothing

Props: Chairs for all players

Goals
- Experiencing mistrust and how it interferes with group spirit
- Dealing with fear, mistrust, and aggression
- Coping with being an outsider
- Integrating the group

How to Play: All players sit in a circle of chairs with their eyes closed. The group leader walks around the circle and quietly taps somebody's shoulder. This player now knows that she is the "wolf in sheep's clothing." The group leader shouts: "All sheep out to pasture!" The players move around on all fours in a circle. Suddenly the "wolf in sheep's clothing" reveals himself, saying "I'm the wolf!" and tries to tag the sheep. They flee to their chairs where they are safe. If they get tagged, they fall down dead.

Variation: Instead of moving on all fours, the players walk around the circle.

Reflections
- What feelings did the wolf and the sheep have? What's the difference?
- In which situations in everyday life are there bad people in disguise?
- Are there people who give you the feeling they are hiding something?
- Are there people who you trust more than others?
- How is trust formed?
- What influence do similar looks, similar clothes, similar manners have on trust?

Role Plays
- You have betrayed my trust!
- If I had known what a phony you are, I wouldn't have trusted you.

- You told someone else the secret I told you yesterday!
- I thought we'd agreed yesterday that none of us would do the extra homework the teacher unfairly imposed on us for punishment. Why did you break our agreement?
- Encounter in a park with a stranger who seems nice, but....

Follow-up Games

82: Vampire and all of its suggested follow-up games

Adding More Imagination

Statue and Sculpting Games
Games 84–92

Fairytale Games
Games 93–96

Pantomime Play
Games 97–101

Frozen Elves

Goals

- Learning to pantomime
- Dealing with the fear of getting caught
- Dealing with false suspicions
- Dealing with exclusion

How to Play: The group is divided more-or-less equally into humans and good elves. The good elves quietly scurry around the room, doing their work in pantomime. They clean, tidy up, and carry objects. Suddenly someone shouts, "The owner is coming!" to signal to the elves that they should freeze and listen. One of the human players then guesses what each elf had been doing when they froze. Then the elves continue working—it must have been the owner's cat they heard! But after some time they hear an ominous sound again, and freeze again, and the next human guesses what they were doing.

Variation: The night when the toys came alive in the toyshop.

Reflection: In which situation in everyday life were you afraid of getting caught?

Follow-up Games

44: Good Morning! ◆ 66: Freeze Tag ◆ 79: Rumors ◆ 85: Spin and Freeze ◆ 93–96: Fairytale Games ◆ 97–101: Pantomime Play

Follow-up Games from *101 More Life Skills Games for Children*

4: Body Language Spells Your Mood ◆ 29: Disposable Secrets ◆ 31: Rumor Factory ◆ 82: Security Guard ◆ 85–90: Statue and Sculpting Games

Spin and Freeze

Goals
- Experiencing cooperation and partnership
- Experiencing body contact
- Renouncing aggression
- Building trust

How to Play: Two players hold each other by both hands and spin around a center like a merry-go-round. At the leader's call, they let go of each other and stop and freeze in a pose. Which of the two is in the stranger position? The people watching can express their opinions, like "You look like a tightrope walker!" or "You look like you're about to take a bow."

Notes
- You need plenty of space to avoid collisions and injuries.
- The two players should be responsible for each other, making sure the other doesn't fall or bump into something.

Follow-up Games
86: Frozen Music ◆ 84: Frozen Elves ◆ 97–101: Pantomime Play ◆ 66: Freeze Tag ◆ 33–40: Working with You ◆ 67: Crocodile Tears

Follow-up Games from *101 More Life Skills Games for Children*
85–90: Statue and Sculpting Games

Frozen Music

Goals

- Learning to sculpt
- Warming up in the group
- Initiating communication and contact
- Improving visual awareness

How to Play: The players move freely to music. They are encouraged to use their whole bodies to make the movements more intense. They should also move their arms above their waistline. When the music stops, they freeze. When they are frozen, they tell the player standing in their line of vision what impression his or her posture makes on them.

Examples

- "You look as if you are running away from something."
- "You look as if you are doing a dance of joy."

Follow-up Games

87: Statue Pairs ◆ 85: Spin and Freeze and all of its suggested follow-up games

Statue
Pairs

Props: Paper and pens/pencils for writing

Goals
- Recognizing social roles
- Recognizing sources of conflicts
- Learning to solve problems
- Improving social awareness
- Developing partner relationships

How to Play: The players are divided into pairs. Every pair writes on a piece of paper two types of people who in everyday life are usually seen together. The pieces of paper are collected by the group leader. Then each pair is given a different piece of paper, sees what people are listed, and puts the paper in a pile on a table. Now, taking turns, every pair poses as statues of the pair written on the paper. The other players try to find the correct slip of paper from the pile that identifies the human statues.

Examples
- Two hospital orderlies
- Conductor and passenger
- Mother and child
- Two boxers or wrestlers
- Two musicians
- Teacher and student
- Dog owner and dog
- Policeman and traffic offender

Variations
- Onlookers give the statue pair an additional task. Example: conductor and passenger. The passenger didn't pay for his train ticket.
- Freeze Tag: a third player shouts "Freed!", and the statues start moving. The two statue figures can now talk to each other; they can leave

together or individually, or say good-by. If the third player shouts: "Freeze!" both freeze in their current position. That way the game can repeatedly be slowed down and speeded up again.

Reflection: Do you know pairs such as these in everyday life who always seem to get along or work together? What conflicts could still occur with such pairs?

Role Plays
- Every pair disagrees.
- Two players are bosom buddies. They praise each other, make promises, and compliment each other.

Follow-up Games
85: Spin and Freeze and all of its suggested follow-up games ◆
86: Frozen Music ◆ 88: Mannequins ◆ 93: Bad News and Good News Pairs ◆ 97–101: Pantomime Play

88

Statue and
Sculpting Games

Mannequins

Goals

- Making nonaggressive physical contact
- Developing social awareness
- Improving visual awareness
- Learning to cooperate

How to Play: Groups of four to eight players are formed. One player is the window dresser. She hauls her mannequins into the window, puts them up, bends their bodies, legs, and arms into shape several times, turns their heads, and adjusts their hands so they can hold something. Several mannequins can also touch each other or form pairs.

The window dresser has to have a specific design in her mind, for example: winter sports, beach goods, or toys.

The other players try to guess what kind of shop it is and what the mannequins are supposed to be doing.

Reflections

- Was it difficult to move the mannequins and bend them into shape?
- How did the window dresser deal with her mannequins? Was she rough or gentle?

Role Play: The less the window dresser uses language to make the mannequins do what she wants, the better she fulfills her assignment.

Follow-up Games
10: Changing the Room ◆ 28: You Sculpt Me ◆ 45–51: Cooperation Games ◆ 89: Wax Museum ◆ 87: Statue Pairs

Follow-up Games from *101 More Life Skills Games for Children*
4: Body Language Spells Your Mood ◆ 35–39: Perceiving You ◆ 52–59: Cooperation Games ◆ 67–73: Relationship Games ◆ 85–90: Statue and Sculpting Games

89

any size

Statue and
Sculpting Games

Wax Museum

Props: Paper and pens/pencils for writing

Goals
- Initiating body contact
- Developing social awareness
- Improving visual awareness
- Learning to cooperate

How to Play: A modeler builds a scene from everyday life using the other students as mannequins—like in a wax museum. First, every player writes on a card what she wants to build. The cards are put in random order on a table. The first player draws a card at random and constructs her scene using as many mannequins as she needs. The scenes can be turbulent, like a bank robbery, or calm, like a café. The other players try to guess what scene is being portrayed by looking for the correct card.

Reflection: Was the scene portrayed by the modeler realistic, original, or funny? Was it the only possible solution? Was it a peaceful or brutal solution?

Follow-up Games
88: Mannequins and all of its suggested follow-up games ◆ 90: Class Picture

Class Picture

Goals

- Getting to know group structures
- Recognizing one's own position in a group
- Training visual awareness
- Being comfortable with some physical contact during group games

How to Play: The photographer asks class members to arrange themselves for the class photo. She requests certain body postures and facial expressions: She gives verbal instructions or walks up to the subjects to adjust their positions.

At the command "Smile!" everybody freezes. When she says "Thank you!" the players can relax and move. They all wander off, chatting to each other. Oops, the photographer forgot to take the picture! They all have to position themselves the same way as before. Does everybody remember where they were standing?

Variations

- A second group is formed that represents the photograph. They position themselves four yards away as a reversed image.
- Several players have the photographer take a picture of their own family. This time they determine for themselves who is to stand next to whom. Every family member should stand in a typical pose so whoever sees the photograph would say, "That's typical!" Another family photo is taken, but the family has just had an argument. The day after that, a group photo is taken during a cheerful outing.

Reflections

- What does your family look like?
- Who would you like to have in your family portrait?
- What can other players spot in the family photo?
- What differences are there between families?

Role Play: The class clown tries to sabotage the picture.

Follow-up Games

91: Acting Out Pictures ◆ 88: Mannequins and all of its suggested follow-up games

Follow-up Game from *101 More Life Skills Games for Children*

88: Family Statues

Acting Out Pictures

Props: Magazines and scissors

Goals
- Illustrating problems and conflicts
- Raising problem awareness and social awareness
- Training visual awareness
- Being comfortable with some physical contact during group games
- Learning to cooperate

How to Play: The players are assigned to look through magazines and to cut out pictures of people in difficult situations (i.e., people fighting, arguing, in danger). In small groups, the situations in the pictures are reenacted either by the players putting themselves in appropriate positions or by choosing one player to act as the "sculptor" of the group (see You Sculpt Me, Game #28). The other players look through the cut-out pictures and try to figure out which one is being reenacted.

Reflections
- What does the picture illustrate?
- What happened before the scene in the picture?
- How could this situation turn out?

Follow-up Games
88: Mannequins and all of its suggested follow-up games ◆ 92: Human Slide Show

92

Human
Slide Show

Props: Illustrated books or magazines

Goals
- Illustrating problems and conflicts
- Identifying problems
- Developing social awareness
- Training visual awareness
- Being comfortable with some physical contact during group games
- Learning to cooperate

How to Play: Players are divided into small groups, and each group looks for an illustrated story in a book or a magazine. Then the individual scenes are constructed. The first "picture" is shown to the other players either by the individual players putting themselves into position or by choosing one player to act as the "sculptor" of the group (see You Sculpt Me, Game #28). The onlookers can comment on the picture or explain what they think is happening. Then he says "Close the curtain!" and the onlookers close their eyes. The performers change their positions, postures, and facial expressions (or are instructed to do so by the "sculptor") and freeze to create the second scene. The onlookers shout "Open the curtain!" and the onlookers open their eyes again. This is how the whole series of scenes or slides is presented.

Variation: Fairytales, myths, and stories from picture books can be presented using this technique.

Note: The slide technique is a very simple drama exercise, which rarely demands too much of the actors.

Role Play: Processing current conflicts and incidents.

Follow-up Games

88: Mannequins and all of its suggested follow-up games ◆ 91: Acting
Out Pictures ◆ 93–96: Fairytale Games

Bad News and Good News Pairs

Props: Paper and pens/pencils for writing

Goals
- Forming pairs
- Finding opposites

How to Play: Players pair off. Every player gets a slip of paper, on which he or she writes down a fairytale figure who is positive. On a separate slip, the partner writes down this figure's antagonist, the negative figure from the same fairytale. These two slips form the "bad news" pair. The players then go on to create a "good news" pair, by thinking of another positive figure from the same fairytale and writing that name down on a third slip of paper.

Examples
- *"bad news" pairs:*
  Hansel—Witch
  Miller's Daughter—Rumpelstiltskin
  Puss 'n Boots—Sorcerer
  Cinderella—Stepmother
  Snow White—Queen
  Little Red Riding Hood—Wolf
- *"good news" pairs:*
  Hansel—Gretel
  Cinderella—Prince
  Snow White—The Seventh Dwarf
  Little Red Riding Hood—Grandmother

Variation: Find positive and negative pairs in everyday life!

Reflections
- Are there fairytales in which there are only positive figures?
- Are there groups of people that have no negative traits?

Role Play: Play short scenes with positive or negative pairs from everyday life!

Follow-up Games
5: The Good Fairy ◆ 39: Twins ◆ 84: Frozen Elves ◆ 87: Statue Pairs ◆ 94: Fairytale Personalities

Follow-up Game from *101 More Life Skills Games for Children*
85: Frozen Pairs

Fairytale Personalities

Props: The completed cards from Bad News and Good News Pairs (Game #93)

Goals
- Linking people with personality traits
- Developing linguistic competence
- Raising social awareness
- Portraying positive and negative relationships
- Recognizing opposites

How to Play: The separated "bad news" slips created in the last game (see Bad News and Good News Pairs, Game #93) are shuffled and handed out. All players then try to find their "bad news" partner. Players can only recognize their partner by hearing a statement that is typical for the character and fairytale. As soon as two bad news partners get together, they start arguing. After arguing for a minute or so, the bad news partners decide to get along with one another again.

Examples
- Hard-hearted (Stepmother)
- Industrious (Seven Dwarves)
- Fearless (Knight)
- Greedy (Wolf)

Variations: The "good news" slips created in the last game are handed out, and each player starts searching for their good news partner. Partners track each other down by making statements typical to their particular character and listening for statements that their partner character might make. When the partners find one another, they are happy and discuss future plans.

Note: For most players, the harmonious positive-positive dialogue is the most boring one. That might also explain why the negative antagonists make fairytales so lively for us. A story becomes exciting when two friends suddenly quarrel with each other, or when a friend becomes a villain, as in the subsequent game.

Follow-up Games
18: Collecting Sound Qualities ◆ 95: Fairytale Surprises ◆ 96: Living in a Fairytale

Follow-up Games from *101 More Life Skills Games for Children*
13–21: How I Am ◆ 35–39: Perceiving You ◆ 46: Punctuation Mark

Fairytale Surprises

Props: The completed slips from Bad News and Good News Pairs (Game #93)

Goals
- Developing emotional awareness
- Reducing prejudice
- Enhancing creativity
- Impersonating aggressive behavior

How to Play: Every player gets an individual slip that was created in Bad News and Good News Pairs (Game #93). Players who receive a positive slip try to find a negative, completely unexpected sentence that this person could say. The players who get a negative slip think of a positive sentence. The other players then try to guess the opposite trait each character has adopted.

Examples
- Snow White says: "The dwarves are really stupid to let me live with them."
- The Witch says: "I actually feel sorry for the two little ones. I will not eat them, I will bake us all an apple pie instead."

Reflections
- Is every person always good or always bad?
- What prejudices do we have about how certain types of characters should act?
- Where do prejudices come from?
- So some people have prejudices against certain looks, professions, or backgrounds?

Variation: The group leader assigns a feeling to each player. Every player then thinks of a sentence that expresses this feeling for his or her fairytale figure, whether the figure is good or bad (a witch can also be happy).

Role Play: In small groups, the players invent fairytales with the same characters but different qualities and feelings. The plot will automatically change.

Follow-up Games
94: Fairytale Personalities and all of its suggested follow-up games ◆
96: Living in a Fairytale

Living in a Fairytale

Props: Texts of fairytales (optional)

Goals
- Dealing with different human characteristics and feelings: fears, sympathy, remorse
- Dealing with conscience
- Reducing aggression
- Developing social awareness
- Learning about dramatic structure

How to Play: Players choose a well-known fairytale and break it down into scenes. They agree on one sentence that summarizes what happens in each scene. With these sentences in mind, they act out each scene either according to the original story or to their own liking, using their imaginations to invent new outcomes. Players should be divided into groups, with enough players in each group to act out all the roles. In the example below there are four characters, so every group would need four players: a mother, a witch, a Hansel, and a Gretel.

Example: "Hansel and Gretel"

Mother: "We have nothing left to eat. We'll leave the children in the woods."

Hansel: "Don't be afraid. I've thrown bread crumbs on the ground so we can find our way back home."

Gretel: "Look, there is a house over there! I wonder who lives in there."

Witch: "Come in. You have nothing to fear."

Witch: "Tidy up the house, sweep the floor!"

Hansel and Gretel: "The witch is dead."

Mother: "I'm so glad you are back!"

Variations
- Then players who are playing the same roles form groups. While cutting

101 Life Skills Games for Children   **165**

wood, the father meets other fathers who have a hard time feeding their kids. While collecting berries, the mother meets other mothers who have worries similar to hers. The children discuss their fate with other children, who are equally afraid of being sent into the woods. In the second scene, Gretel can appear with several personalities: as anxious Gretel, as high-spirited Gretel, as confident Gretel, or as simple-minded Gretel. What personalities could Hansel have? The third scene can be dealt with in a similar way.

- In the fourth scene, the parents can appear in the background (as their conscience) and comment every now and then on what is happening.
- In the fifth scene, Gretel could act rebelliously and the witch could try to beg for mercy.
- In the sixth scene, Hansel and Gretel could seesaw between joy, remorse, and sympathy. Maybe the witch's ghost appears?
- In the seventh scene, Hansel and Gretel return to their father as adults. They now see everything from a different perspective.

Role Play: Attempt a contemporary version of the fairytale

Note: It is not just classic fairytales, and certainly not just the Hansel and Gretel story, that are suitable for this method. Anything from a modern novel to a picture book can be the basis for this game. The advantage of fairytales is that many children know the storylines. However, the group leader should make sure that any story they choose is known by all of the players. If that is not the case, the leader should tell the story to the group before starting the game.

Follow-up Games
94: Fairytale Personalities and all of its suggested follow-up games ◆
95: Fairytale Surprises

Getting Stronger

Goal
• Learning to cooperate

How to Play: The players stand in a circle. Using pantomime, everyone bends down and pretends to lift a heavy sheet of glass together. The hands of all players have to take hold of it at the same distance from the floor. They carry the plate glass a few yards. It has to stay the same size.

Variations
• All players unroll a huge canvas.
• All players pull on a long rope as if they were pulling against an imaginary opposing team in a game of tug-of-war.

Reflections
• What was difficult about doing this activity together?
• Did people make mistakes? Why do mistakes happen?
• In which everyday activities do you need the help of other people?
• Did you feel comfortable in this game or was it unpleasant for you?
• With which persons would you like to play this game in a small group?
• Could this game work in your family?

Role Plays
• The family is carrying a huge rubber dinghy to a beach far away.
• Two student groups play tug-of-war in pantomime. The first prize is an additional week of vacation. Why did one group lose?

Follow-up Games
50: Tug of War ◆ 97–101: Pantomime Play

Follow-up Games from *101 More Life Skills Games for Children*
All suggested follow-up games for 52: Come into the Circle

Unpacking a Gift

Goals
- Being patient
- Being creative
- Expressing oneself without words
- Interpreting nonverbal behavior

How to Play: The players take turns taking an imaginary gift out of an imaginary box in the middle of the room. The other players guess what the gift is from the way the player handles it and from their facial expressions.

Variation: Instead of the players thinking up their own gifts, they could pick a slip of paper from a bowl of prompts written out by the leader.

Example: A player "receives" a tennis racket as a gift.

Follow-up Games
29: You Reflect Me ◆ 74: Slo-Mo Tennis ◆ 78: Peace Language ◆ 84–92: Statue and Sculpting Games

Waiter

Goals
- Being creative
- Expressing oneself without words
- Interpreting nonverbal behavior

How to Play: In this game the players create a restaurant scene that can include diners (both children and adults), a maître d', waiters, and a chef. Making sure the players use pantomime and do not talk, the diners are welcomed, seated, and served food and drinks from a tray. Players who are diners at the restaurant then pretend to eat and drink what they are served.

Variation: Players can take turns serving and being served. They can pretend to be satisfied or can make a big row about how bad the food or service is.

Follow-up Games
29: You Reflect Me ◆ 74: Slo-Mo Tennis ◆ 78: Peace Language ◆ 84–92: Statue and Sculpting Games

Flying Masks

Goals
- Being creative
- Expressing oneself without words
- Interpreting nonverbal behavior

How to Play: A player makes a funny face that represents a mask and then "takes off the mask" by running his hand over his face. With a movement of the hand, he throws it to another player in the circle. She catches the mask, with a movement of the hand puts it on, changes it, and throws it to someone else.

Follow-up Games
29: You Reflect Me ◆ 74: Slo-Mo Tennis ◆ 78: Peace Language ◆
84–92: Statue and Sculpting Games

any size

Pantomime Play

Mime Chain

Goals
- Being creative
- Expressing oneself without words
- Interpreting nonverbal behavior

How to Play: Four players leave the room. The others agree on an action that is to be portrayed in pantomime by one person. The first of the four waiting players is called in. Without knowing what the portrayed action is supposed to be, she watches with interest and interprets the action. Now she calls in the second person and shows him, in her own pantomime, what she has seen. Then it's the second person's turn and then finally the third person's turn. The last player guesses what the action is supposed to represent.

Follow-up Games
29: You Reflect Me ◆ 74: Slo-Mo Tennis ◆ 78: Peace Language ◆
84–92: Statue and Sculpting Games

Follow-up Game from *101 More Life Skills Games for Children*
4: Body Language Spells Your Mood

Keyword Index

accusation, 79

acoustic perception, 14–19, 55

affection, 52, 58, 61–63, 65–67, 73, 78

aggression, 17, 28, 43, 47, 52, 55, 61, 63, 64, 67, 71, 73–75, 77, 81–83, 85, 88, 95, 96

aggression-free body contact, 52, 61, 63, 67, 71, 88

behavior (social), 44, 78, 87, 95, 99

blindness, 31, 52, 53, 55, 81, 82, 83

boasting, 6, 56

change, 5, 8, 10, 100

characteristics, 18, 42, 53, 54, 95, 96

clichés 87, 94

closeness 20–23, 27–45, 52, 55, 71, 75, 77, 79, 80, 94, 95

communication, 20–44, 46–49, 52–56, 57–63, 67, 68, 70, 71, 73, 78, 80, 86, 87, 93, 94, 97–101

competition, 36, 40, 50, 60, 69, 72, 74, 77

concentration, 8–19, 29, 46, 55, 84, 95, 97–101

conscience, 76, 84, 96

consideration, 33, 37, 40, 42, 52, 55, 71, 74, 96

consolation, 58, 59, 62

contact (personal), 2, 11–13, 18, 19, 20–27, 30, 41, 43, 44, 46, 52–56, 57–61, 78, 80, 86,

conversation, 54, 56, 58, 70, 78, 86, 94

cooperation, 27–40, 45–51, 57, 64–66, 68, 69, 72, 77, 85, 87–89, 91–94, 96, 97

coordination, 34, 35–38, 69, 77, 89, 91, 92, 96

creativity, 5, 10, 18, 19, 22, 26, 36–38, 43, 52, 59, 62, 63, 68, 70, 73, 78, 85, 86, 88, 89, 92, 95, 96, 97–101

dependence, 34, 35, 36, 57, 60, 64–66, 68, 69, 85

dexterity, 34, 36–38, 40, 51

disability, 6, 7, 64

dislike, 4, 5, 77–79

distance, 37, 77, 79, 80

doing without, 3

exam, 60

fairness, 40, 74, 79, 81

fear, 60, 64, 71, 75, 76, 79, 81–84

fear of entering, 52–55, 71, 79, 81

flexibility, 10, 58, 59

generosity, 3, 62

gestures, 46, 60, 78, 98–101

getting to know each other, 1–7, 20–32, 41, 52–54, 56

gifts, 3, 62, 98

greeting, 25, 43, 44, 46

group spirit, 8, 42–44, 45, 48–51, 52, 53, 56, 60–62, 64–66, 68, 70–73, 75, 77, 83, 84, 88–90, 97

guessing, 7, 12, 13, 17, 18, 19, 68, 78, 84, 98, 101

guilt, 76, 79, 84

helping, 34, 50, 57–68, 72

honesty, 6, 54, 56, 60, 78

inhibitions, 41, 43, 44, 73

integration, 26, 35, 45, 52–56, 57, 58, 64–66, 71, 72, 83

introducing oneself, 1–7, 27, 41–44, 52, 54, 56

leading, 29, 37, 68

losing, 36, 40, 50, 57, 64, 66, 69, 72, 74

memory. *See* remembering

movement, 2, 29, 31, 33–35, 37, 38, 41, 42, 45, 46, 48, 50, 61, 64–69, 71–77, 81–86, 97, 99, 100, 101

music, 1, 16–19, 29, 31, 37, 41, 43, 44, 45, 47, 86

noise, 14–19, 47, 55, 61, 77, 81, 82

objects, 9, 11, 12, 15, 49, 62, 68, 70, 97–101

observation, 8–19, 29, 30, 52, 53, 55, 78, 85–92

opposites, 6, 11, 53, 77, 87, 93–95

outsiders, 58, 72, 79, 80, 83

pairing off, 19, 28–40, 57, 58, 69, 77, 81, 85, 87, 93, 94

pantomime, 7, 68, 84, 97–101

partnership, 19, 21–40, 45–56, 57, 58, 63, 65–69, 73, 85, 87, 93

patience, 51, 67, 68, 74, 88, 98, 101

peace, 78

performance, 7, 35, 36, 40, 45–51, 60, 69, 72, 74

physical contact, 25, 28, 31, 32, 34, 35, 38, 42, 43, 45, 52, 55, 61, 63–67, 71, 73, 74, 81–83, 85, 88, 89, 91, 92

pictures, 1, 3–5, 59, 62, 70, 91, 92

positive thinking, 5, 80

problem awareness, 56–59, 87, 91, 93–95

questions, 54, 58, 60

reducing aggression, 17, 47, 74, 75, 81, 96

relaxation, 31, 32, 41–44

remembering, 2, 11–19, 23, 41, 55, 90

renouncing aggression, 28, 43, 55, 71, 73, 74, 77, 81, 85,

secrets, 20, 54, 76, 84

self-awareness, 1–7, 8, 27–32, 76, 79, 80,

self-esteem, 6, 7, 36, 48–51, 60, 72, 79, 80

self-image, 1, 54, 56, 79, 80

sensitivity, 28, 29, 31, 32, 37, 52, 56, 57–59, 62, 68, 71, 78, 79

shapes, 12, 28, 49

social awareness, 7, 39, 44, 53, 54, 57–59, 61, 62, 78, 80, 87–89, 91–94, 96, 99

solidarity, 8, 45, 50, 53, 57–59, 62, 64, 66, 67, 72, 77, 97

speed, 2, 35, 36, 42, 45, 48, 61, 64, 65, 66, 67, 69, 74, 83, 100

strength, 50, 64, 65, 72, 97

summoning, 26, 63,

tactile awareness, 11, 12, 32, 71

tolerance, 40, 51, 58, 73

touching. *See* physical contact

trust, 6, 20, 28, 31, 32, 33–37, 52–55, 57, 58, 61, 64, 65, 67, 71, 73, 81, 83, 85

visual awareness, visual perception, 1, 7, 8–11, 13, 25, 27–30, 33, 39, 53, 68, 78, 85–92, 98, 100, 101

warming up, 2, 17, 37, 41–44, 61, 86

waking someone, 52

weaknesses, 6, 54, 56, 58, 59, 64–67, 72, 74

winning, 35, 36, 40, 50, 57, 64, 69, 72, 74

wishes, 3, 70

you-relationship, 20–40

The Games Arranged by Specific Categories

Advanced Games

19: Song Memory
30: You Draw Me
39: Twins
40: Fair Ball
58: The Comforter Game
68: Moving Help
76: Detective
79: Rumors
82: Vampire
91: Acting Out Pictures
92: Human Slide Show
96: Living In a Fairytale
101: Mime Chain

Games Requiring a Large Space

33: Holding Me with Your Eyes
50: Tug of War
55: I'm Here!
64: Bodyguards
65: Brother, Help! Sister, Help!
66: Freeze Tag
67: Crocodile Tears
69: Carrying Contest
72: Tug of War II
82: Vampire
85: Spin and Freeze

Games Not Requiring Props

2: The Run-to Game
6: I Can, I Can't
7: Guess What I Can Do
8: Observing the Room
10: Changing the Room

11. What's Made of This?
20. Traveling Names
28: You Sculpt Me
29: You Reflect Me
32: When It Rains, It Pours
33: Holding Me with Your Eyes
36: New World Record
37: Dance Partners
38: Patty-Cake
39: Twins
43: Greeting Game
44: Good Morning!
47: Boom Box
52: Wake Up!
53: The Grouping Game
55: I'm Here!
61: Cry for Help
63: I Fell in the Well
64: Bodyguards
65: Brother, Help! Sister, Help!
66: Freeze Tag
68: Moving Help
69: Carrying Contest
71: Animals in the Jungle
74: Slo-Mo Tennis
75: Polite Wild Animals
77: Frontline
79: Rumors
80: Praise
81: Ghosts and Travelers
82: Vampire
84: Frozen Elves
85: Spin and Freeze
86: Frozen Music
88: Mannequins
90: Class Picture
97: Getting Stronger

98: Unpacking a Gift
99: Waiter
100: Flying Masks
101: Mime Chain

Games Not Requiring Physical Contact

1: I Like This Picture
3: Wishing Cards
4: Evil Fairy's Hat
5: Good Fairy
6: I Can, I Can't
7: Guess What I Can Do
8: Observing the Room
9: The Room's ABCs
10: Changing the Room
11. What's Made of This?
13. A Piece at a Time
14: Seeing with Your Ears
15: Telling Noises Apart
16: Stand Up for Your Instrument
17: Telling Sounds Apart
18: Collecting Sound Qualities
19: Song Memory
20. Traveling Names
21: Crossword Puzzle Names
22: Gathering Names
23: Autograph Book
24: Building Names
26: The Seat on My Right Is Empty (with a Twist)
27: I Met My Match
29: You Reflect Me
30: You Draw Me
33: Holding Me with Your Eyes
36: New World Record
37: Dance Partners
39: Twins
40: Fair Ball

41: Balloon Dance
44: Good Morning!
46: Take a Bow
47: Boom Box
48: Beat the Clock
49: Building Skyscrapers
50: Tug of War
51: Paper Streamer
53: The Grouping Game
54: Hot Seat
56: Information Please
57: Solution Memory
58: The Comforter Game
59: The Helper Game
60: Friendly Exam
62: Emergency Kit
68: Moving Help
69: Carrying Contest
70: First Day of School
72: Tug of War II
75: Polite Wild Animals
76: Detective
77: Frontline
78: Peace Language
79: Rumors
80: Praise
84: Frozen Elves
86: Frozen Music
87: Statue Pairs
90: Class Picture
93: Bad News and Good News Pairs
94: Fairytale Personalities
95: Fairytale Surprises
96: Living In a Fairytale
97: Getting Stronger
98: Unpacking a Gift
99: Waiter
100: Flying Masks
101: Mime Chain

SmartFun activity books encourage imagination, social interaction, and self-expression in children. Games are organized by the skills they develop, and simple icons indicate appropriate age levels, times of play, and group size. Most games are noncompetitive and require no special training. The series is widely used in schools, homes, and summer camps.

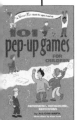

101 RELAXATION GAMES FOR CHILDREN: Finding a Little Peace and Quiet In Between by *Allison Bartl*

The perfect antidote for unfocused and fidgety young children, these games help to maintain or restore order, refocus children's attention, and break up classroom routine. Most games are short and can be used as refreshers or treats. They lower noise levels in the classroom and help to make learning fun. **Ages 6 and up.**

>> 128 pages ... 96 illus. ... Paperback $14.95 ... Spiral bound $19.95

101 PEP-UP GAMES FOR CHILDREN: Refreshing, Recharging, Refocusing by *Allison Bartl*

Children get re-energized with these games! Designed for groups of mixed-age kids, the games require little or no preparation or props, with easier games toward the beginning and more advanced ones toward the end. All games are designed to help children release pent-up energy by getting them moving. **Ages 6-10.**

>> 128 pages ... 86 illus. ... Paperback $14.95 ... Spiral bound $19.95

101 QUICK-THINKING GAMES + RIDDLES FOR CHILDREN
by *Allison Bartl*

The 101 games and 65 riddles in this book will engage and delight students and bring fun into the classroom. All the games, puzzles, and riddles work with numbers and words, logic and reasoning, concentration and memory. Children use their thinking and math and verbal skills while they sing, clap, race, and read aloud. Certain games also allow kids to share their knowledge of songs, fairytales, and famous people. **Ages 6-10.**

>> 144 pages ... 95 illus. ... Paperback $14.95 ... Spiral bound $19.95

101 MOVEMENT GAMES FOR CHILDREN: Fun and Learning with Playful Movement by *Huberta Wiertsema*

Movement games help children develop sensory awareness and use movement for self-expression. The games are in sections including reaction games, cooperation games, and expression games, and feature old favorites such as Duck, Duck, Goose as well as new games such as Mirroring, Equal Pacing, and Moving Joints. **Ages 6 and up.**

>> 160 pages ... 49 illus. ... Paperback $14.95 ... Spiral bound $19.95

101 MUSIC GAMES FOR CHILDREN: Fun and Learning with Rhythm and Song *by Jerry Storms*

All you need to play these games are music CDs and simple instruments, many of which kids can make from common household items. Many games are good for large group settings, such as birthday parties, others are easily adapted to classroom needs. No musical knowledge is required. **Ages 4 and up.**

>> 160 pages ... 30 illus. ... Paperback $14.95 ... Spiral bound $19.95

101 MORE MUSIC GAMES FOR CHILDREN: New Fun and Learning with Rhythm and Song *by Jerry Storms*

This action-packed compendium offers musical activities that children can play while developing a love for music. Besides concentration and expression games, this book includes relaxation games, card and board games, and musical projects. **A multicultural section** includes songs and music from Mexico, Turkey, Surinam, Morocco, and the Middle East. **Ages 6 and up.**

>> 176 pages ... 78 illus. ... Paperback $14.95 ... Spiral bound $19.95

101 DANCE GAMES FOR CHILDREN: Fun and Creativity with Movement *by Paul Rooyackers*

These games encourage children to interact and express how they feel in creative ways, without words. They include meeting and greeting games, cooperation games, story dances, party dances, "musical puzzles," dances with props, and more. No dance training or athletic skills are required. **Ages 4 and up.**

>> 160 pages ... 36 illus. ... Paperback $14.95 ... Spiral bound $19.95

101 MORE DANCE GAMES FOR CHILDREN: New Fun and Creativity with Movement *by Paul Rooyackers*

Designed to help children develop spontaneity and cultural awareness, the games in this book include Animal Dances, Painting Dances, Dance Maps, and Story Dances. The **Dance Projects from Around the World** include Hula Dancing, Caribbean Carnival, Chinese Dragon Dance, and Capoeira. **Ages 4 and up.**

>> 176 pages ... 44 b/w photos. ... Paperback $14.95 ... Spiral bound $19.95

101 LANGUAGE GAMES FOR CHILDREN: Fun and Learning with Words, Stories and Poems *by Paul Rooyackers*

Language is perhaps the most important human skill, and play can make language more creative and memorable. The games in this book have been tested in classrooms around the world. They range from letter games to word play, story-writing, and poetry games, including Hidden Word and Haiku Arguments. **Ages 4 and up.**

>> 144 pages ... 27 illus. ... Paperback $14.95 ... Spiral bound $19.95

101 DRAMA GAMES FOR CHILDREN: Fun and Learning with Acting and Make-Believe *by Paul Rooyackers*
Drama games are a fun, dynamic form of play that help children explore their imagination and creativity. These noncompetitive games include introduction games, sensory games, pantomime games, story games, sound games, games with masks, games with costumes, and more. **Ages 4 and up.**

>> 160 pages ... 30 illus. ... Paperback $14.95 ... Spiral bound $19.95

101 MORE DRAMA GAMES FOR CHILDREN: New Fun and Learning with Acting and Make-Believe *by Paul Rooyackers*
These drama games require no acting skills — just an active imagination. The selection includes morphing games, observation games, dialog games, living video games, and game projects. A special multicultural section includes games on Greek drama, African storytelling, Southeast Asian puppetry, Pacific Northwest transformation masks, and Latino folk theater. **Ages 6 and up.**

>> 144 pages ... 35 illus. ... Paperback $14.95 ... Spiral bound $19.95

101 IMPROV GAMES FOR CHILDREN AND ADULTS
by Bob Bedore
Improv comedy offers the next step in drama and play: creating something out of nothing, reaching people using talents you don't know you possess. With exercises for teaching improv to children, advanced improv techniques, and tips for thinking on your feet — all from an acknowledged master of improv. **Ages 5 and up.**

>> 192 pages ... 65 b/w photos ... Paperback $14.95 ... Spiral bound $19.95

YOGA GAMES FOR CHILDREN: Fun and Fitness with Postures, Movements and Breath
by Danielle Bersma and Marjoke Visscher
A playful introduction to yoga, these games help young people develop body awareness, physical strength, and flexibility. The 54 activities are variations on traditional yoga exercises, clearly illustrated. Ideal for warm-ups and relaxing time-outs. **Ages 6–12.**

>> 160 pages ... 57 illus. ... Paperback $14.95 ... Spiral bound $19.95

THE YOGA ADVENTURE FOR CHILDREN: Playing, Dancing, Moving, Breathing, Relaxing *by Helen Purperhart*
Offers an opportunity for the whole family to laugh, play, and have fun together. This book explains yoga stretches and postures as well as the philosophy behind yoga. The exercises are good for a child's mental and physical development, and also improve concentration and self-esteem. **Ages 4–12.**

>> 144 pages ... 75 illus. ... Paperback $14.95 ... Spiral bound $19.95

Mandalas represent wholeness and life. Their designs and patterns are taken from geometry, nature, and folk art. Made up of simple elements, yet often marvelously complex, they fascinate children and adults alike. Mandalas have been found in prehistoric caves, ancient tapestries, and the art of people all over the world. These three mandala books make wonderful gifts for children and parents, and can be used anywhere — all you need is a set of colored pens, pencils, or crayons.

42 INDIAN MANDALAS COLORING BOOK
by Monika Helwig

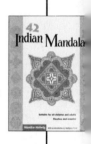

Traditionally made of colored rice powder, flowers, leaves, or colored sand, mandalas such as the ones in this book have been used to decorate homes, temples, and meeting places. They may be used daily as well as on special occasions, and are found in the homes of people of all faiths. Each pattern is different and special, increasing the delight of all who see them.

42 MANDALA PATTERNS COLORING BOOK
by Wolfgang Hund

The mandalas in this book mix traditional designs with modern themes. Nature elements such as trees and stars reflect the environment, while animals such as fish, doves, and butterflies remind us we are all part of a universal life. Motifs repeat within mandalas in a soothing way that encourages us to revisit the images, finding new shapes and meanings in them each time. A perfect introduction to the joy of coloring mandalas.

42 SEASONAL MANDALAS COLORING BOOK
by Wolfgang Hund

The seasonal and holiday mandalas in this book will appeal to both the sophisticated and the primal in all of us. Luscious fruit, delicate flowers, leaves and snowflakes are among the nature designs. Holiday themes include bunnies and jack-o-lanterns, Christmas scenes, and New Year's noisemakers. Children can learn about the seasons and celebrate familiar holidays with these playful designs!

>> All mandala books 96 pages ... 42 illus. ... Paperback $11.95

101 FAMILY VACATION GAMES: Having Fun while Traveling, Camping or Celebrating at Home by Shando Varda

This wonderful collection of games from around the world helps parents to connect with their children. Full of games to play at the beach, on camping trips, in the car, and in loads of other places, including Word Tennis, Treasure Hunt, and Storytelling Starters.

>> 144 pages ... 7 b/w photos ... 43 illus. ... Paperback $14.95 ... Spiral bound $19.95

Free shipping on all personal website orders